FLASHES OF MEMORY

*A Childhood among the
Clyde Lighthouses*

Mary Gillanders

FLASHES

OF

MEMORY

A Childhood among
the Clyde Lighthouses

Thanks and acknowledgements

I owe a debt of gratitude to Millport Museum (Museum of the Cumbraes), which holds the diaries of Mary Ann Wodrow. Extracts of these are used by their kind permission.

The archivists there also directed me to James Blake's excellent book *Lighthouses on the Clyde*.

I would like to thank my three sisters, with whom I share happy memories of loving parents. To them and to the memory of my parents, this memoir is affectionately dedicated.

Light-hearted Memories

Time seems to pass too quickly,
A swiftly-ebbing tide;
Fond memories stir within me
Of those beacons on the Clyde.

Bright beams sweep over water
Calm in the evening air,
Recalling sweet days of childhood
And part of me lingers there.

Registered Charity SC047866

First published in 2020 by Acair,
An Tosgan, Seaforth Road, Stornoway, Isle of Lewis, Scotland HS1 2SD

info@acairbooks.com
www.acairbooks.com

Text and cover design by Margaret Ann MacLeod, Acair

A CIP catalogue record for this title is available from
the British Library.

Printed by Hussar Books, Poland

ISBN: 978-1-78907-047-7

CONTENTS

THE END OF AN ERA

The 31st March 1998 has a special place in our memory. On that day, Her Royal Highness Princess Anne attended a poignant ceremony on remote Fair Isle in the Shetland Isles. Watched by the Princess and an interested crowd from far and near, the lighthouse keepers at the Fair Isle South lighthouse lowered the flag of the Northern Lighthouse Board for the last time, thus marking the final automation of all lighthouses in Scotland.

A fine plaque, unveiled by Her Royal Highness, commemorates 'the invaluable services of generations of lighthouse keepers from 1787 to 1998'. Later that year the North Foreland lighthouse in England was automated and thus a distinctive and honourable way of life in the nation had come to an end. It was a nostalgic and, for some, a sad occasion that triggered many memories. As my father was a lighthouse keeper, my entire childhood was spent on lighthouses – but the days of lighthouses as we knew them are over.

For 211 years the Northern Lighthouse Board, with headquarters in Edinburgh, had been responsible for the oversight and maintenance of most of the lighthouses, from Muckle Flugga in Shetland to the Calf of Man, the southernmost lighthouse on the Isle of Man, over 200 in all. Princess Anne, as patron of the Northern Lighthouse Board, has long taken a keen interest in the lighthouse service and has visited many of their stations

Visits now would be different. Without people, without welcoming and knowledgeable keepers in smart uniform, without the happy shouts of children, without trim, well-kept buildings and grounds, without, it may be, the sense of remoteness, so much else is missing – the sense of man and the elements now in opposition, now working in harmony, now at peace. That was the world of my childhood and the world I remembered when the flag was lowered at Fair Isle South.

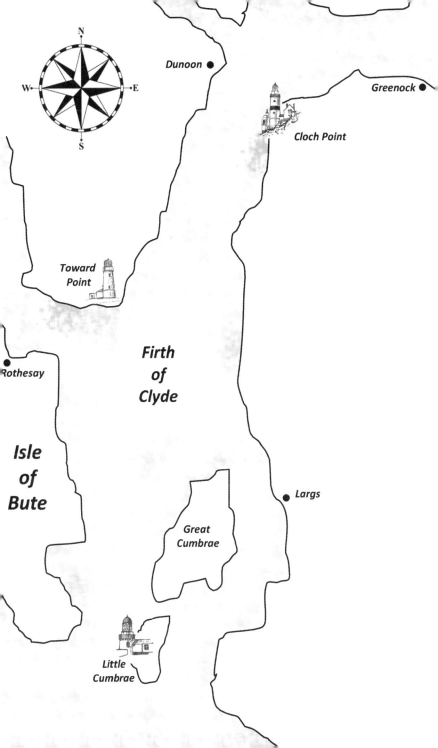

Chapter One
WELCOME TO WEE CUMBRAE

There are three lighthouses in Scotland that do not come under the jurisdiction of the Northern Lighthouse Board and it is on these that we as a family look back with affection. The Clyde Lighthouses Trust (CLT) was the authority responsible for those at Cloch, Cumbrae and Toward Point, on the inner Firth of Clyde, and for the maintenance of all navigational aids from Little Cumbrae northwards to Ardross, while the Clyde Navigation Trust was responsible for the river channel on to Glasgow.

As a young man in the 1930s, my father applied to the trustees of the CLT and, after an interview, was appointed second assistant keeper on Little Cumbrae lighthouse. He had spent some time at sea, so was already knowledgeable about wind and waves and the handling of boats.

Little Cumbrae – or Wee Cumbrae, as it is perhaps more popularly known – lies in the Firth of Clyde between the Isle of Arran to the west and the Ayrshire coast. It is a rugged little island just under one mile wide and almost two miles long. Great Cumbrae – or Big Cumbrae – is one and a half miles to the north across the stretch of water known as the Tan. To the south the Firth opens out with Ailsa Craig on the horizon, half-way to Ireland.

The name of the island has appeared under various forms – *Cumaradh Beag* (Gaelic), *Kumbra Beg*, *Little Cumray*, *Lesser Cumbrae*, *Little Cumbrae* – but to us it was always Wee Cumbrae. Some say the name means a 'shelter' or 'refuge', others say it means 'steep'. Many of its place-names are Gaelic in origin while others show a Norse influence.

Each lighthouse had a principal keeper, a first assistant and a second assistant. The principal keeper, as might be expected, had the overall responsibility, but otherwise the men shared tasks equally and in our experience seemed to work harmoniously together. The policy of the CLT was that the keepers should move among the three stations as dictated by the exigencies of men leaving or retiring and others entering the service. The exception to this was that they were never required to spend more than five years at a time on Wee Cumbrae, perhaps because there might be problems for some families – for example children's schooling – or perhaps because the island had an undoubted charm and all must get their fair share!

On all three stations the routine was basically the same with local variations. The men were on three-hour shifts round the clock – three hours on duty followed by six off. When there was fog the shifts were of six hours' duration – three hours tending the light followed by three in the engine room, where the huge engines that provided power for the foghorn were housed. Lighting-up time, of course, varied with the time of year. Winter brought long working nights for the keepers lasting from lighting-up shortly after 3pm till around 9am.

From Monday to Friday the men were on duty from 9am till noon. Records and charts were checked and equipment was tested. The mirrors or prisms surrounding the light were cleaned to a sparkling polish and preparations made for the evening's lighting-up. Vaporised paraffin was used in Cumbrae and Toward lighthouses for the light, both in the tower and in the houses, so the mantles had to be checked or changed, a delicate operation as they were so fragile that at the first opportunity they broke or snagged. Everything pertaining to lighthouses was particular, meticulous, trim. All brasswork shone. The grounds were kept spick and span. Gravel pathways were regularly raked and freshened and lawns were smoothly green with clean-cut edges.

Tuesdays, Thursdays and Saturdays were 'boat days' when the keepers took it in turn to sail to Millport on Big Cumbrae for supplies – that is, weather permitting! Armed with large basket and shopping lists the keeper made his way along Guildford Street to butcher, baker, dairy and Post Office. It was a welcome social outing as they got to know many of the townsfolk, some of whom became lifelong friends. When the weather was favourable, the women could enjoy a shopping trip too.

It was only in very adverse weather that a trip was cancelled. There were cases, naturally, when the weather deteriorated suddenly, or the wind changed direction unexpectedly. In doubtful conditions the womenfolk would be advised: "No, it's not the day for a trip. It'll be rough enough going, but coming back ...... No, no; better put it off today." They usually, and wisely, obeyed orders! It could be distracting for the boatman if passengers were showing alarm, or giving advice, though the men were invariably understanding.

On one such day two workmen were to be picked up in Millport. One lady, from the confines of the

My father Roderick MacCuish, as a young man in the 1930s,
second assistant keeper at Little Cumbrae lighthouse.

On warm summer days the women-folk might make their
way down to Steadholm Bay. I am on the left.

Dad with myself (right) and my sister, and the big
shopping basket, on a shopping trip to Millport.

The big rock on Cumbrae, the place for
picnics, barbecues and sitting in the sun.

The lighthouse tender vessel CLT *Torch* was our means of
moving house, transporting not only personal items, but the
families as well. The crane at wee Cumbrae came into its own
as, one by one, heavy items were winched down the cliff face.

Views of Cumbrae lighthouse, showing the clifftop
position and the extent of the keepers' domain.

The lighthouse tender vessel CLT *Torch*.

A much later view of Cumbrae lighthouse.

The island of Little Cumbrae from the air, with the lighthouse doman in the foreground.

sheltering lighthouse wall, maintained: ''No, it's a fine day; it's not stormy at all. I'll be all right!" and insisted on going. As predicted the return trip was very choppy and, as the boat lurched up and down and the wild spray flew, her cries of alarm were enjoyed by the boatman; "Stop, stop! You'll have us all drowned! Turn back! You're drowning us!" "No, no!" the boatman assured her: "It's a fine day! Not stormy at all, calm as can be!"

Afternoons were free till lighting-up time. In his free time the keeper tended his garden; potatoes, carrots, leeks, cabbage and celery grew in abundance. Apple and plum trees lined the back wall of the complex while blackcurrants and gooseberries ripened in the sheltered gardens. The men took pride and pleasure in their gardening and would have understood the feelings of an early 19th century keeper who, when reconstruction to Cumbrae lighthouse took place throughout the summer season, put in a claim for 'want of garden' and was awarded compensation of £5!

The men had the routine of work and the sharing of responsibilities and decision-making that went with it, but it might seem a lonely life for the women-folk. Not so; on warm summer days they might make their way down to Steadholm Bay. As they sat, backs against the sheltering Big Rock, they knitted or sewed and chatted with day-trippers from Millport, while their little ones swarmed around and over 'the mountain'. And there were two goats and sundry hens to appease!

A pleasant afternoon's outing was to pay a visit to the families over on the farm side of the island. A well-marked path climbed up the hill and near the top there was the temptation, not to be resisted, to sit on an inviting rock and admire the wonderful view of Bute away to the right, with the Arran hills and Brodick directly opposite, and Lamlash nearer the south end of the island with Holy Isle just off it and the Firth opening out beyond. Below, not much is happening; a keeper is carting seaweed up for his garden, a kestrel swoops past, a skylark trills close by. Peace!

Five years passed quickly and it was time for my parents to leave for Cloch lighthouse. The move would be accomplished with the aid of the *Torch*, the sturdy 310-ton vessel which was the tender of the CLT. It would head out from the CLT's private wharf at Port Glasgow for Cumbrae. With family and baggage safely on board it would leave with a goodbye hoot of the horn as they began a new chapter in a new home.

Chapter Two

A GLIMPSE INTO THE PAST

Everybody knows that the first lighthouse, as far as can be ascertained, was the Pharos of Alexandria in Egypt, built around 300BC and famous as one of the seven wonders of the ancient world. Not everyone, however, knows that Scotland's first lighthouse was built in 1635 on the Isle of May in the Firth of Forth and was tended by a lone keeper.

The fuel used for the light was coal, so every few days the supply boat would arrive and tip its load into the shallow water at high tide. When the tide had receded, the keeper would retrieve the coal and manhandle it to the base of the tower whence it would be winched in a bucket to the grate at the top. His annual pay was £7. Added to that were unlimited fishing rights and 30 bushels of meal for his family, who were housed on the mainland. When he was still working into his eighties, the authorities took pity on him and supplied a horse as a burden-bearer and an assistant keeper as a burden-sharer!

By the early 18th century, trade with the American colonies was increasing and so sea traffic switched to Scotland's rugged west coast. Ever more ships were making their way upriver from the Firth of Clyde to Greenock. These sailing ships were largely at the mercy of wind and tide as well as having sandbanks and hidden reefs to contend with. The frequency of accidents gave rise to much concern – it was reckoned that up to a thousand deaths a year were due to shipwreck. Action was required.

After much discussion and delay, finally in early 1756 an Act of Parliament decreed that a lighthouse be built on "*the Island of Little Cumray in the County of Bute ...... for rendering the navigation in the Frith and River of Clyde more safe and commodious*" and assent was obtained, from "*Our Sovereign Lord GEORGE the Second, by the grace of God, of Great Britain, France and Ireland, King.*"

Thus was formed the Cumray Lighthouse Trust. A year later, there was the lighthouse perched on the highest point of the island, 409ft (121m) above sea level and, for the privilege of using his ground, an annual fee of £2 was paid to the Earl of Eglinton, owner of the island.

Under the instructions of James Ewing, the tower and a modest cottage for the keeper were built, possibly of local stone. It must have been a considerable undertaking to transport building materials and equipment from the shore where they were landed on the east side of the island. It is likely that ponies or donkeys were used for carting goods up the hill and over rock and bracken to the flat area at the top.

The circular tower is 30 feet in height. Inside can still be seen the remains of the spiral stairway that led up to an iron grate which held the '*coalls*' which, when lit, told mariners approximately where they were. Coal came from the Cambuslang mines on the outskirts of Glasgow. We can picture horse-drawn carts bumping their way over the moorlands of Ayrshire towards Irvine, which was a busy commercial port in those days. From there progress would be by barge over the twelve nautical miles to the eastern side of the island and so up to the lighthouse. It was then the lighthouse-keeper's task to hump the coal up the winding stair to the top of the tower.

From records we learn that in 1759 the cost of 100 cartloads of coal, inclusive of transport, was £10 16s. It seems that 545 carts of coal were ordered in one particular week, but we are not told how long that amount would last. Of course, it might well have been a case of stockpiling lest stormy weather should later prevent barges from delivering supplies.

This first tower at Wee Cumbrae must have given a very fitful light. Storms blew, rain poured down and fog obscured though, since the Cumbraes are in the path of the North Atlantic Drift, snow seldom blanketed the island. However, reliable or not, shipmasters sailing to Ireland or the British ports were grateful for it, even though the trustees levied dues from all shipping that "*do pass or repass*" the lighthouse. Incidentally, lighthouses down the years continued to be funded entirely by dues payable by all ships that passed through British waters.

The original two light keepers "*at present residing on Cumray*" were Peter Montgomerie and Thomas Fairie, with a remuneration of £15 for their services from December 1757 to Whitsuntide 1758. However, this was obviously given with a grudge as records show: "*the wages are by much too high and the Trustees should look out for a fitt person who will serve at a reasonable wage and live near the lighthouse*".

Two keepers were replaced by one, a certain David Pollock. His wage, from Whitsuntide 1758 to Whitsuntide 1760, was £29. Forty years later his son, also David, who succeeded him as keeper, was receiving £31 10/-. When he died in 1804 his widow was appointed keeper of the Cumbrae light on the grounds that she had virtually had the responsibility of the lighthouse when her husband become incapacitated in his later years. Interestingly, some American lighthouses, up until 1929, were tended by women.

A quotation from CLT records of 1857 has a certain warmth about it: "*I find from the Minute Book that at the term of Whity* (Whitsuntide) *1828, the Trustees, in respect of her advanced age and long and faithful services, Resolved to allow Mrs MacLean a superannuating allowance of £20 per annum. This allowance she enjoyed for very nearly 29 years, having died at the advanced age of 106 years on Jany last. With your Lordship's concurrence I paid her Grandchildren the current half-year's annuity.*" For comparison, records tell that in 1794 the going rate for men-servants on Big Cumbrae was £6 to £8 a year. It has been suggested that this Mrs MacLean was David Pollock's widow and that she remarried. If so, it seems that the CLT were generous to this last serving member of a family who, for almost seventy years, had tended the light-on-the-hill followed by the light-on-the-clifftop.

Glasgow magistrates watched Greenock's mounting prosperity with envy and made up their minds that the river must be deepened and made navigable right up to their own city. Naturally the merchants of Greenock thought otherwise! Already their rivals had attempted to attract trade by building a pier at what became the town of Port Glasgow, with its own custom house.

By 1790, with faster ships and the Clyde ever more busy, it had become apparent that, from every point of view, safety arrangements were inadequate. On clear nights the coal-fired light on Wee Cumbrae might have been reasonably visible, but if the prevailing south-westerly winds were blowing the flame would flicker erratically. A complete reappraisal was undertaken. The problem was looked at from every angle. What should take the place of coal? Candles? Oil? Should the existing lighthouse be adapted? Were, in fact, two lighthouses required on the island? The sea-going fraternity were consulted widely.

A sailor's life was a peculiarly precarious one. To the vagaries of wind and weather on the ocean expanse were added the dangers of hidden reefs, rocky coasts and frequent collisions as ships negotiated narrow channels and silted-up rivers. To these natural risks were added press-gangs, pirates and the despicable wreckers who, from the safety of shore, helped themselves to the bounty of the ships they lured to their doom.

It was at this time that the CLT became involved in a consultative capacity with the Stevenson family, renowned lighthouse builders – an association that was to continue for the next 150 years. Robert Stevenson, born in 1772, was the son of a Glasgow merchant, Alan Stevenson, who died when Robert was an infant. A few years after her husband's death his widow and her young son moved to Edinburgh. He was a bright lad and his mother was intent on giving him the best education she could afford.

When Robert was 15 she married a widower, Thomas Smith, engineer to the recently-formed Northern Lighthouse Board. He owned an ironware business and had a special interest in lighting; he it was who designed the street lighting for Edinburgh's New Town. During holidays from Glasgow University, Robert helped out, became interested and gladly switched his university studies from Latin, Greek and theology to engineering. When the CLT contacted the commissioners of the NLB for advice, the 19-year-old Robert was entrusted with the design and building of a new lighthouse on Little Cumbrae and began making plans.

He built his first lighthouse on a plateau on the south-west corner of the island, where it still stands in a commanding position on the edge of a 100ft cliff. The tower was 36 feet high – not much taller than the earlier tower – and the all-in cost was £1,000. The light shone out for the first time on 1st October 1793, at first a fixed light but later with its distinguishing double flash every 30 seconds. It was a good starting point from which to develop the skills that were to see Robert become a master of lighthouses and the founder of a dynasty.

Thomas Smith had designed a method of lighting using oil lamps and, as coal was no longer considered efficient, oil from Greenland sperm whales was used for the light. Then, in 1823, there was a further upgrade when 15 argand lamps were installed. These were oil lamps with glass funnels, the invention of a Swiss scientist, Ami Argand, and they gave a better, purer light which was reflected by a series of silvered mirrors. Whale oil was later abandoned in favour of rapeseed oil, which was found to be cleaner and more economical.

Later on, vaporised paraffin and, later still, gas and finally electricity came into use. In 1974 the lighthouse became fully automatic.

Robert Stevenson next set his sights on a much more formidable undertaking. With engineer John Rennie he went on to build the Bell Rock lighthouse in the North Sea, 12 miles off Dundee on the east coast of Scotland. In old times the monks of Arbroath Abbey had installed a warning bell on the rock – hence the name. It doubtless was the means of saving some lives, but nevertheless wrecks occurred at the rate of six a year on average. In 1804 the battleship *HMS York* hit the rock with the loss of 500 lives. It was time for action.

Robert spent three arduous years on the rock with his men, three years during which he lost three of his children, back home in Edinburgh, to whooping cough. The 130ft slender tower first shone out on 1st Feb 1811, a worthy monument to skill, imagination and courage.

In 1797 he had married Jean Smith, daughter of his stepfather. A grandson, Robert Louis, later described her as a loving mother who diligently read her Bible and had a sense of humour which she kept under firm control! Of their nine children, four died in childhood. Three sons, Alan, David and Thomas, qualified as civil engineers and went on to design and build lighthouses. Alan, with a love of classics and the arts – he was a friend of Wordsworth – is famed for the soaring Skerryvore out in the Atlantic Ocean, 12 miles west of the island of Mull, while David was entrusted with the impossible-looking Muckle Flugga. Two of his sons, David and Charles, followed in their father's footsteps and built many of the lights that increasingly, year by year, seemed to spring up to warn mariners of the hazards of the Scottish coast. Charles's son, D Alan Stevenson, born in 1891, carried on the family tradition into the fourth generation of the Lighthouse Stevensons.

Thomas's only son, Robert Louis, was employed in the firm, too, but only for a reluctant three years as he served his apprenticeship on the Dubh Artach among other lights before declaring, much to his family's disappointment, that he was going to follow his dream. Off he went to pursue a successful career in writing novels, poetry and thrilling tales about his travels – and avid readers of *Treasure Island, Dr Jekyll and Mr Hyde* and *Kidnapped* are glad that he did.

However, words he wrote in 1880 reveal his pride in his forebears' achievements: "*Whenever I smell salt water, I know that I am not far from one of the works of my ancestors. The Bell Rock stands monument for my grandfather, the Skerryvore for my uncle Alan and when the lights come out at sundown along the shores of Scotland, I am proud to think they burn brightly for the genius of my father.*" The opening lines of one of his poems might suggest that he felt slightly regretful that the writer's life that he had chosen was less worthy than theirs.

> "*Say not of me that weakly I declined*
> *The labours of my sires and fled the seas.....*"

The CLT's association with the Stevenson Civil Engineering Firm lasted until 1952, when Mr D Alan Stevenson retired. He died in 1971. The Stevenson family had been a crucial force in the building of a hundred lighthouses round the coasts of Scotland with the consequent saving of innumerable lives – a noble legacy.

Records pertaining to lighthouses are full of fascinating detail. Among a set of instructions for the keepers of the Bell Rock Light, issued in 1823, are the following which perhaps give a flavour of life at the sea-front at the time:

"Daily allowance per man: 1 lb Beef; 2oz Oatmeal; 2oz Barley; 2oz Butter; 3 quarts Beer; Vegetables and salt, no stated allowance; for tea and other necessities, 4d per day."

Rules are set to govern and advise many aspects of their lives:

"The light-keepers be cleanly in their persons and linens, and proper in their apparel in general."

"The light-keepers are enjoined to assemble in the Library, for the purpose of reading the Scriptures, and for Prayers, every Sunday, at 12 o'clock noon, in their Uniform-dress. This

service is to be performed by the Acting Principal Light-Keeper, or Principal Officer of the Board present. The table is to be covered during this service with a flag; and, when the weather is moderate, the Lighthouse flag is, at the same time, to be hoisted to the mast head, and allowed to remain till sunset."

"Pay attention to Strangers, showing them every civility in their power; and particularly, to afford their aid and assistance, in case of shipwreck; yet so as not to neglect anything incumbent upon them, in the proper discharge of their duty as light-keepers."

Soon after the establishment of Little Cumbrae lighthouse, there were calls for another light, but where, exactly? A committee reported in 1795 that they had:

"visited the Cumbray Light house, which was in very good order although they have not a very favourable opinion of the person who lights it."

After much deliberation and changing of minds it was decided that a lighthouse should be built at Cloch Point, five miles from Greenock. The Stewart family of Ardgowan willingly agreed to the use of their land.

Work commenced immediately and Cloch Lighthouse became operational in 1796, ultimately flashing once every five seconds. The original tower had one dwelling attached to it and the solitary keeper would seem to have earned his reasonable wage of £36 a year. A second keeper was appointed about 1850 and later a third.

Meanwhile negotiations were ongoing about a lighthouse at '*Towart Point*' on the southern tip of the Cowal peninsula. It was lit in 1812 on ground belonging to the Lamonts of Knockdow. Like Cumbrae and Cloch, this lighthouse was built by Robert Stevenson. Its flash was at ten-second intervals. The CLT became responsible for these three with two unmanned lights – one on the Gantocks, an underwater rock off Dunoon, and the other at Garroch Head on the island of Bute.

By this time James Watt of Greenock and others had seen the possibilities of using steam as power and Henry Bell's Comet, the first viable steamship, sailed the same year as Toward lighthouse was built. Twenty years later over thirty steamers were plying the waters of the Clyde. By mid-century there was an emphasis on speed which was measured by the time taken to 'run the lights' – from Cloch lighthouse to the Cumbrae light.

Hundreds of ships passed the three Clyde lighthouses, but only one Iron Church! When the Church of Scotland split in 1843 in what became known as the Disruption, most of the congregation of Strontian on the west coast joined the newly-formed Free Church. They approached Sir James Riddell, the land-owner, for a site on which to build a church. He resolutely refused their request, so they had to worship in the open air in all weathers. Then someone had a bright idea: "We can't build on land. Let's have a church on the loch!" In no time money had been collected while a firm in Greenock undertook the construction. In July 1846 down the Clyde it sailed, sitting on a platform towed by two tugs and gazed at by wondering crowds. It was towed all the way to Strontian where it was awaited with joyful anticipation and doubtless a degree of curiosity. The floating church was anchored on Loch Sunart, some 150 metres offshore. It served as a place of worship, with services in Gaelic and English, and on weekdays as a school, till 1873.

The increase in traffic was welcome. Accidents, however, were frequent despite the considerable improvement in safety and Cumbrae, positioned in the middle of the estuary, witnessed many. In 1856, on a night of thick fog, the steamship *Albion*, on its way from Stranraer to Glasgow, was badly damaged when she went aground 200 yards from the lighthouse. The lighthouse authorities were concerned. What to do about fog? As usual they talked to the very people who might have ideas – those '*who go down to the sea in ships.*'

They took time to mull over the various options – bells, horns, trumpets – and finally decided on a tried and tested horn system already adopted at Dungeness by Trinity House, the authority responsible for English lighthouses. The inventor, an American by the name of Daboll, offered his expertise for the sum of £600 and he even came from New York to oversee the installation. It consisted of a calorific engine, a device in which air is repeatedly heated and cooled in a cylinder. The resulting expansion and contraction drives a piston which compresses the air blown through the foghorn to produce the distinctive drone.

Just as each light had its distinguishing pattern, so had each fog-horn. Cumbrae's fog signal alternated two blasts of one and a half seconds with three of two and a half seconds, at intervals of 35 seconds. The system was copied in the other two lighthouses with slight differences, the duration and frequency of blasts identifying the lighthouse to the sea-going fraternity. While Toward gave one three-second blast every 20 seconds, Cloch gave blasts of one and a half seconds every 50 seconds. The installation of the foghorns prompted the keepers to ask for an increase in wages, as they were now expected to be engineers as well as lighthouse keepers!

Now that it had three lighthouses with fog-horns, plus the Gantocks and Garroch lights, the Clyde was well prepared for the boom days that were to come. Year by year more, larger and faster steamships were setting out for the Americas and the colonies for tobacco, tea, cotton and much more. The upshot was that, with these safety features in place, there was a domino effect of increased traffic reaching upriver as far as Glasgow, bringing in turn yet more work, trade and prosperity, while ship-yards were building yet more ships. In 1871 an Act was passed, giving to the body now to be known as the Clyde Lighthouses Trust the responsibility for lighting, upkeep of buoys and dredging of the river from the southern point of Cumbrae and virtually all the waterways north, including the various lochs and channels.

While use of steam grew in importance, sailing ships were by no means outmoded. Clippers vied for the China tea trade and with a fair wind made good speed, besides being a delight to behold. The *Ariel* was hailed as '*the fastest thing on water.*' The *Cutty Sark*, built in Dumbarton, first cut through the waters of the Clyde in 1870 and for the next seven years was engaged in the China tea trade before switching to the wool trade with Australia. She now attracts thousands of admirers to Greenwich every year.

And yet there were accidents. A sailing ship, the *Lady Isabella*, was facing a rising storm as she sailed into the Clyde estuary on a wild August day in 1898.

As the wind tore at her sails and the waves buffeted her, the sailors battled to keep her off the shores of Wee Cumbrae. In spite of their desperate struggles the gale drove the ship relentlessly on and hurled her on to the jagged rocks just south of the lighthouse. The crew managed to get a rope to the shore and, though they escaped with their lives, the ship was a total wreck.

In January 1931 the Stevenson family made a further contribution to safety at sea when Alan Stevenson installed a talking beacon at Cumbrae lighouse. It was the first lighthouse in Scotland to use the device, followed by Cloch lighthouse. Its purpose was to enable ships with radio direction finding equipment to pinpoint their position in relation to the lighthouse and it proved especially useful in fog. A gramophone record gave the name of the lighthouse and counted from one to thirty and so the operator on ship was able to get his bearings. All depended on the difference between the speed with which sound travels and that at which wireless waves travel. From the time difference between the arrival of each at the ship, the distance from the lighthouse could be calculated.

Two months later, on 21st March 1931, the passenger liner *Montclare* was returning from Canada when she encountered thick fog on entering the Firth and reduced speed to a minimum. Suddenly passengers were aware of a heavy grinding as the ship struck rocks not far from the lighthouse. The light keepers, of course, were involved in giving any help they could. Tugs and so on arrived and, after several unsuccessful attempts to free the ship, the 300 passengers were transported to Largs. At high tide the lightened ship was successfully towed off the rocks. The damage sustained was minor and she was eventually back in service.

For decades, the lighthouses of the Clyde flashed and sounded out their warnings to mariners in darkness, in fog and in storm. The sea continued to take its toll.

Chapter Three

CLOCH LIGHTHOUSE

Cloch is an anglicised form of the Gaelic cleuch or clach meaning 'the big stone'. The lighthouse stands 76 feet high – well short of the tallest lighthouse in Great Britain, Skerryvore, standing at 138ft. Cloch may not be singularly tall but it is undeniably a handsome structure, especially when viewed from the sea. Its tall, slender frame then stands silhouetted against the greenery and rocks behind, with a distinctive black band round the white tower.

In contrast to Wee Cumbrae, Cloch lighthouse was situated by a relatively busy road that ran down the coast to Largs and Wemyss Bay, with buses passing between Largs and Glasgow. Directly across the Firth of Clyde is the Argyllshire town of Dunoon, while Gourock and Greenock were a short bus-ride away. Butcher, grocer and fishmonger, each with his van or horse-drawn cart, called regularly and onion johnnies on bicycles arrived in autumn. Hawkers, too, came calling, cases packed with clothes or ribbons, threads and needlecraft sundries.

It was at Cloch that I made my début. A nurse in white uniform had moved in and ruled our household with a rod of iron. Mother was superbly cared for while children (and father) were kept firmly in their place. An older sister recalled how on B-day Dad took all four girls up to Holmes' Farm for the daily pail of milk. On their return, Nurse met them at the door, hands on hips.

"Well, can any of you guess what I've got for you upstairs? No? Come along then, wash your hands and I'll show you."

Four big sisters clustered to view the new baby. Now we were *five*. My sister remembered her bewildered reaction to this latest addition to the family.

"I don't understand. You put on your wellingtons to go for the milk ….and when you get back….there's a baby in the house….and anyway….what has it got to do with washing your hands?"

My memory of our life at Cloch is very hazy. Any

account inevitably relies on my sisters' reminiscences, so what follows is a medley of memories.

We were in one of the two-storey semi-detached houses, which have attractive crowstepped gables. An early first impression is of the black range in the living-room, glowing coals showing through the bars and a kettle humming on top of the grate. The words 'black lead', 'pipe clay' and, especially, 'Brasso' spring to mind. On the wall on either side of the mantle-piece, gas-lamps with glass funnels caught the light from the window that looked out on to the road down the coast to Largs and Wemyss Bay. The other window faced north. On winter mornings those windows wore a magic tracery by the artist Jack Frost – every morning a different pattern, which gradually disappeared as the fire in the grate burned bright.

Next door were Mr and Mrs Walker from the Isle of Man. The steps leading down from the road were wide and topped by a handsome wrought-iron gate. They were opposite Mrs Walker's doorway and she took pleasure in keeping them clean and attractive-looking; the edges decorated with pipe-clay swirls and twirls as on her own front step. We appreciated the result and somehow it epitomised the proper pride the keepers took in their surroundings.

While Daddy Walker (as we named him) was genial and kindly, Mrs Walker was not averse to showing her displeasure when we thoughtlessly messed up her handiwork. Yet it was she who nurtured our sister's interest in gardening as together they planted pansy seeds in the garden opposite the engine room.

Near the engine room was the wash-house which the women were free to use on their allotted day. In one corner the large boiler, heated by a coal fire, appeared to be encased in concrete. The double sink was divided by a large mangle and there were washing boards, poles, ropes, irons and suchlike paraphernalia. Washing was hung out to dry on the shore where poles were set into concrete just left of the big gate at the bottom of the path.

Next to the wash-house were one or two store-rooms and the coal-shed, where the men helped themselves to as much coal as they could use. My sister remembers seeing Mr Scott coming up with two big pails of coal. The seven-year-old thought: "Oh, I must help Daddy Scott with his coal!" She ran out to take hold of a handle and with pails duly dumped by his door step he thanked her: "That was a great help; don't know how I'd have managed without you" and off she skipped.

There we saw snow for the first time. One morning we opened the door and before us lay a new, glistening, pure white world. We stood on the doorstep entranced. The snow was deep, possibly two feet deep, and it looked so soft and springy, just like our beds upstairs.

With a whoop we threw ourselves down and – fell right through! After that came the fun of snowball fights with the children next door, rides on improvised sledges and a snowman complete with keeper's cap.

Winter was hardly fun for the keepers. Getting up at midnight at the call of a bell to face an icy gale was one of the lesser attractions of their calling. On the other hand, there were few experiences that could match the joy of an early dawn in April, when the birds poured out their song to celebrate a new day and the air was fresh and free.

One morning we heard the greeting: "Fine morning, Willie!" "Aye, spring in the air, Roddy!" and all was activity. We came home from school to find men in dungarees carrying pails, ladders, brushes with an air of purposefulness. Men from the works in Port Glasgow had arrived and platforms were suspended around the lighthouse. As work proceeded we wondered at how the new white was even whiter than white. Trimmings such as window-sills were a mid-grey and there might be a touch of black here and there as on railings.

There were five Scott children, of whom the youngest three were roughly our age. In summer we were out all day. We spent hours on the shore, paddling, climbing, playing at wee houses, gathering pebbles and shells; followed by ball games, leap-frog, peever, building dens – testing ourselves, using our imagination. No one seemed to worry about what we were getting up to – or they would have put a stop to some of it, especially to the thrill we got from another ploy. The lighthouse stood on a rock over which the sea washed constantly. At very low tide we would pick our way round the base to the other side – for a new view of the world! But only once or twice – it was too scary. The flat roof of the engine room with its parapet was another temptation – even at risk of a well-deserved scolding.

When the seashore palled there was the lime-pit. Whitewash was used on the enclosing wall and unused lime ended up in a hollow in the rock. We were told it was dangerous – it would burn us, keep away! So off we went to verify. It did look sinister, smoke rising, bubbles plopping. Over the months it hardened and we dared to leap across it, hair standing on end at the thought of falling in, for we thought it was fathoms deep under the top crust.

We joined up with Jean at Cloch Ferry for ploys down by the old jetty; wandered in Bluebell Wood in happy Maytime; built castles on the wide sands at Lunderston Bay, gathered brambles and, one memorable day of golden sun, accompanied Dad up the path to Barber's Farm and beyond to pastures new, where we sat on a grassy bank longing to know what lay beyond the gentle hill that touched the intense blue sky.

On one or two afternoons during the week the lighthouse was open to visitors. We youngsters, too, enjoyed the occasional trip to the top, exclaiming at the different views from each successive window on the way up, up, round and round the winding stairs to the light-room. From the balcony the view suddenly widened to reveal a river that was like a doorway to the world.

Then school intervened. With Nancy, Robert and Wilma from next door we piled on to the bus that passed the lighthouse at 8.20 every morning. Invariably one or more of us would be missing as the bus appeared round the bend and the shouts would go up: "Here's the bus! The bus! Hurry!" and round the corner and up the steps the stragglers would fly, certain the bus would take off without them.

One sister remembers: "We went to Gourock Eastern School, which was a seven-teacher school with a headmaster – master, of course! Schooldays were as happy as they are said to be. The 'please-misses' were strict, too strict perhaps, but on the whole kindly. Desks were in rows facing the blackboard with teacher perched on a stool at her high desk. The strap was used for minor offences which perhaps forestalled major. Few escaped without experiencing the 'Hold out your hand!' order.

"Our Primary IV teacher was rather formidable. One whisper and you found yourself caught by the shoulders and shaken vigorously, head flopping up and down. Nevertheless, she was conscientious and we respected her. For spelling homework we wrote out the ten most difficult words from our reading portion and laid the list on our desks. Miss would perambulate, picking up one strip of paper here and another there. One evening I wrote the ten longest words; next evening eight-letter words; the next seven, six, five, four and then, with some trepidation, three. No repercussions! I dared two – 'by, to, ox ...' and sat, list on desk and eyes likewise. Suddenly I was being shaken violently to the familiar: "Isn't that the limit? Isn't that the limit?" Well, I guess it was.

"We took for granted the thoughtfulness shown by our teachers. One winter, I remember, we went along to the staff-room at dinner time to collect mugs of cocoa to take back to our room, quite on the teacher's own initiative. They even took us to their homes when our bus failed to appear or went sailing past. One wintry afternoon our fearsome Primary IV teacher took us to her house to await the next bus. The first surprise was that she actually had a house. We had the half-formed idea that teachers were firmly attached to school. And there was another lady there – old, too, (by our reckoning). And our teacher was different, more like an 'ordinary' lady. We had a drink and biscuits and an exciting story to tell when we got home.

"The school sat at the corner of a crossroads, so many of the children had at least one road to cross. Traffic was sparser then and lollipop men had not yet been invented. Safety was our own responsibility. Mrs Barr's sweetie shop across the road was a magnet to those fortunate few with the necessary coinage to patronise it. The two or three rows of jars on the shelves behind the high wooden counter, filled with all colours of sweets, were purely to be admired by us scholars. Rather, depending on means we decided: "H'penny tray, please" or "Penny tray, please" and out from beneath the counter came the relevant tray. We waited with infinite patience while the purchaser carefully considered whether to have a penny dainty, or a liquorice pipe, or maybe a liquorice strap or what about a sherbet poke? He picked up a gobstopper... no, he'd have two from the h'penny tray! The whole experience was exciting and Mrs Barr just stood there and let us take our time.

"My primary VII class was entirely different from my experience of school hitherto. Our teacher was young, fresh out of college *and* she did not wear a smock! And in some lessons, like sewing, we were even allowed to talk! And, unbelievably, if we had finished our sums quickly and correctly, we could occupy ourselves quietly in any way we pleased – drawing, handwork, reading a book from the small class library. Or she might give us an extra-hard arithmetic problem just as a challenge. It felt like the beginning of a new era in education."

But by that time the country was already in the midst of war.

Chapter Four
WARTIME

On 3rd September 1939 war was declared on Germany. At first nothing much happened and then things began gradually to change. We came home from school one day to find our gleaming white lighthouse in battle-dress – a sludgy green and khaki – and we learned a new word – camouflage.

The garrison on the hilltop behind the lighthouse became a reality to us. We had known it was there but, as it was forbidden territory and we very seldom, if ever, saw anyone going in that direction, it had figured little in our consciousness. Then suddenly there were soldiers everywhere. The lighthouse was on a strategic point between the military fort on the hilltop across the road and the boom defence laid to trap any German U-boat daring to venture up the River Clyde. On both counts it was vulnerable to attack. The road was cordoned off in both directions so that there was no entry to the lighthouse environs. Sentry boxes were posted at intervals – at Cloch Ferry, then another halfway to the lighthouse, another at the beginning of the lighthouse wall, one at each of the three gates and so on to Lunderston Bay and beyond. A sentry with bayonet fixed on rifle stood, seemingly motionless, in each. Barrage balloons floated in the sky above.

Buses from Gourock were allowed no further than Cloch Ferry and similarly from the other direction all traffic was cut off. So now of a morning we galloped to The Ferry and there we were dropped again on the way home. Coming home, especially in winter when darkness fell early, presented a problem – better to tip-toe past the sentry, hoping he pays no attention, but risk startling him into shooting us? Or tramp, tramp so that he gets time to see that it's just us? I remember coming home with Mum one moonlit evening and the challenge ringing out: "Halt! who goes there?" I suppose the sentries were on alert – or perhaps they just liked to practise on us for their own amusement.

The lighthouse was effectively sealed off – no more butcher's van or hawkers. Ration books were issued

Cloch lighthouse. Built at Cloch Point and operational from 1796, it was an undeniably handsome structure and the place where I was born.

The lighthouse was five miles from Greenock
and it was here that we spent the war years,
with shipping coming and going along the Clyde.

Cloch lighthouse.

and after school on Thursdays we collected our weekly allowance of butter, sugar and sundries from the Co-op in Gourock – and received change from our ten-shilling note! It seemed as if everything was rationed. Winston Churchill refused to countenance the rationing of tea, insisting that the British housewife simply could not be deprived of 'the cup that cheers'. However, tea was ultimately rationed, as well as cheese and ham and soap and meat and ...and ...and. Bread escaped rationing, at least for a while, but loaves became greyer and greyer. We became acquainted with dried eggs and dried milk, but with home baked scones and oatcakes, homemade jam, vegetables from the garden and milk from Holmes' Farm we were never hungry. I remember when meat and fish had run out we occasionally had mashed potato and milk for our evening meal and we loved that, probably for its novelty value.

Our grandfather from the Highlands sent us a gift of mutton – in fact a whole sheep's carcass – by rail and when it arrived at Gourock the stationmaster contacted Dad. But how to get it home? Baby was duly ejected from her pram and Mum set off on the three-mile walk to town. On reaching the station she enjoyed the banter – and envy – of the railway staff as they tenderly tucked the sheep into the pram and sent her merrily on her way. Back at home we watched with interest as Dad sharpened his knives on the whetstone and divided the meat into chops, roasting portions and boiling bits for 'sheep's heid broth'. In the absence of freezers meat was preserved in salt. The suet was set aside for a 'clootie dumpling' which we regarded as a great treat.

We were issued with gas-masks, which thankfully we never had to use; trying them on for practice was bad enough. We had air raid practice, too, because although the raids almost always took place at night there was always the risk of a day-time attack and we had a few, though they may have been false alarms. An air-raid shelter stood in the upper playground. The siren would sound and out the children would march to the shelter to await the long continuous blast of the 'all clear'. My teacher would lead us in singing 'It's a long way to Tipperary' and 'We'll hang out our washing on the Siegfried Line.' She laughed a lot and told jokes – I wondered how she dared!

We children were very conscious of how the war was proceeding. I remember being told about the surrender of France and the retreat from Dunkirk. We must have picked up from overheard discussions that the situation was critical. We could picture so vividly the 'little ships', the bombs, the heroism, the tragedy. We also heard snatches of Churchill's stirring speeches.

I've a clear memory of glancing, late one afternoon, out of an upstairs bedroom window. To my amazement the roadway was thick with people trudging stolidly onwards and past us, some pushing prams piled high, some with sacks on their backs, children holding on to parents or big brothers, all looking weary and downbeat. They were making for Lunderston Bay where scores of tents were provided. On enquiring what was happening, Mum told me that they were survivors from the previous night's bombing. The road may have been specially opened for them, or possibly they were victims of the very early raids before defensive plans were put into effect.

Blackout was strictly observed. The Clyde was a prime target for the Luftwaffe and air raids became more frequent. Immediately there was a warning, the light in the tower was extinguished. We were advised to shelter in the walk-in cupboard under the stone stairs, as that was reckoned to be the strongest part of the house. We would be not long in bed before, about a quarter to nine, we would hear the distinctive vroom-vroom-vroom which told of approaching planes, on their way to wreak devastation on the Clydeside shipyards. I lay one night thinking: "It's about time for them – hope they don't come – they're not coming tonight…" and right then, on cue came the familiar sound, faint but relentlessly coming our way. All three keepers were immediately out on duty.

Soon we were advised that if the lighthouse suffered a direct hit we would be trapped where it would be very difficult to reach us. So henceforth we were to shelter in the living room. The two outer walls each had a large window with heavy wooden shutters held shut by brass clasps, so that they did not let out a glimmer of light. During a raid we dragged the table to the corner by the pantry and lay down under it – a better idea than it seems, for the road above our level acted as a buffer. Now the thuds of bombs and crackle of gun-shots from the anti-aircraft battery above sounded louder and the shudder as they landed more earth-shaking.

There had been night after night of bombing. One morning we found our school standing amidst the rubble of shattered buildings. One tenement had its frontage blown off and, on the remaining part of the second-storey floor, a vase stood intact on a small table. A boy from my class was missing and we soon heard the story. During the night the siren had sounded and he alone of his family had gone down to the air-raid shelter. His tenement had taken a direct hit and the young lad had lost his whole family. We saw him no more as he went to live with his grandmother on the Island of Bute.

The Clydebank Blitz occurred on Thursday 13th and Friday 14th of March 1941, when the town suffered the worst bombardment of any city in Britain. Bombs rained down all night long and the devastation was terrible. Mercifully, we knew little of its full extent. Fire raged for days and only seven houses remained unscathed.

About six weeks later, on the evenings of the 6th and 7th May, came the Greenock Blitz. My sister remembers: "I can vividly recall that night – the wailing of the siren, the horrible tension, then the drone of the German bombers, the whine of the falling bombs. On top of the hill across the road was a military fort, so we were well aware of our unenviable position. Dad was up in the tower and later he described the scene to us. The planes flew down the river towards the lighthouse, dropping bombs – one – two – three... the next, he thought, would hit the tower...he was sure we were all about to die.

"In the house there were some moments of confusion. We were huddled together under the substantial kitchen table, which at least gave a feeling of protection. The heavy wooden shutters were suddenly blown open by the force of an explosion. Up shot my sister and tried to shut them but the bolt had gone. She promptly turned off the light. I thought her wonderfully brave. I myself was full of despondency. I was sure Hitler would get us and I was scared because

I wasn't ready to die. I prayed that somebody would kill Hitler and so end this terrible war. All the evil in the world was bound up in him."

A day or two later, we all walked down to Lunderston Bay and saw the crater left by that fourth bomb.

There was a submarine base at the nearby Holy Loch. The Clyde shipyards were busier and more vital than ever and vulnerable to German U-boats, so a boom defence had been laid from the foot of the lighthouse tower across to Dunoon on the opposite bank. It was basically a strong steel curtain stretching down from large floats possibly down to the seabed. From the shore it gave the appearance of giant stepping stones across the river. The boom-ship was constantly opening and closing the curtain to let convoys, destroyers, battle-ships pass through, besides the steamers following their busy timetables.

One night we were kept awake, not by bombs this time but by a constant deep *boom*, *boom*, *thud*, overlaying a medley of noise. The whoosh of depth charges continued all night.

In the morning the shore – our shore – was covered with layers of fish, some even landing in the garden above. All along the beach in both directions the fish lay, torn to bits. It was suspected that a German U-boat was trying to penetrate the boom defence. We never heard anything further than that.

And yet with all this in the background it is amazing how carefree we were. We went to school as normal, the only concession being that, after a raid, school opening was deferred till 10 o'clock.

By this time we had new neighbours. Mr and Mrs Sinclair came from the Isle of Man. Mary, gentle and quiet-spoken, had the distinction of having been tennis champion of her home island. Archie was rather short and slight and inevitably was referred to, among the workmen, as 'Wee Archie'. Whenever I heard someone being called 'a real gentleman' I thought of Mr Sinclair, in the first memory I have of realising what was meant by the term *gentleman*, though I could not have explained why.

Being sparse of hair Archie always wore his cap for protection against sun and wind. Always, except when he came into the house, when unfailingly off it came to rest on the dresser as, bent over the wireless, he and Dad did their best to coax sound out of it, sometimes successfully, even if spasmodically. There was much discussion of accumulators and their woefully capricious ways.

Coming off watch at six o'clock one winter's evening, Dad met Archie. They were two of a kind and that afternoon Archie was bent on mischief and Dad was going to enjoy it too! Earlier that afternoon Archie was out of cigarettes and had asked his wife to walk the short distance to the hotel to buy some. Not averse to a bit of genial company Mary set off and spent some time (a long time!) chatting to the owner's wife. In her absence Archie had fretted and fumed and he and the sentry on duty hatched a vengeful plan. Waiting in the shadows with Dad, Archie listened for the sound of his wife's footsteps while the sentry stood to attention at his post.

"Halt! Who goes there?" The sentry's shrill voice cut the night air.

"It's only me!" came the timid reply. "It's ...it's Archie's wife!" and Mary made to pass. Her way was promptly barred by the sentry's fearsome bayonet.

"There's a woman here who claims to be your wife. Can you identify her?" he demanded of Archie, urging the hapless victim forward. From the shadows Archie denied all recognition.

"My wife went up to the hotel hours ago. Never clapped eyes on this woman. Take her away!"

There followed much expostulation from the direction of the sentry box, then a plaintive wail. "Oh Archie, I *am* your wife! Don't be silly. There's a war on, don't you know!"

Always one to have the last word, Archie growled: "You're telling me there's a war on! You'll know that when I get you home!"

The three men took leave of one another in great spirits, feeling a little more than satisfied with their evening's diversion. Even wartime had its lighter moments!

Because of restrictions imposed by wartime rationing, many commodities had all but disappeared from the shops. One morning the three keepers appeared carrying crates of oranges which had been washed in on the tide, probably from the cargo of a vessel that had foundered. Much of the fruit was saturated beyond use, but a quantity was retrievable. It was quite a find, so the womenfolk used their ingenuity and limited ingredients to produce several welcome jars of marmalade and chutney, not at all unpalatable, even if not up to WRI standards! Although we were appreciative of the sea-bounty, we knew all too well that it came at a cost. Much the same thing happened on the island of St Kilda, though it was said that the St Kildans: "gathered the oranges and boiled them, fried them, stewed them, but found them still inedible!"

The war had not yet come to an end when once again it was time for us to be on the move. We were heading back to Cumbrae, which sister Flora half-thought belonged to her, since she was one of the few people to be born on the island in modern times *and* on the late Queen Mother's birthday! When the National Anthem was played on 4th August, she told her gullible wee sisters that it was in her honour. How could we doubt it?

Chapter Five
CUMBRAE LIGHTHOUSE

Our move to Cumbrae took place in autumn when the bracken turns golden and the nights draw in. During my childhood I sampled all three lighthouses, but it is Cumbrae lighthouse that has a special place in my heart. As always, the family and all our belongings were being transferred by the *Torch* and, as we neared the landing site and I looked up, up to the wall and tower on the dark cliff-top, I knew this was *home*. We made our way to the steps that climbed steeply to the plateau above – all 69 of them! A chain grab-rail on the edge nearer the shore gave a sense of protection. At the top, the view that met us was surprisingly green and pleasant.

On the grassy plateau, the spacious lighthouse grounds were enclosed by a high whitewashed wall. Attached to the lighthouse were two semi-detached houses while a third house, ours, was a pleasant bungalow-type building on the perimeter wall. As at all three stations the sturdy stone-built houses were roomy and furnished. Each keeper had his own garden, drying green, hen-house and even a byre – but no cow, and a pig-sty with no pig! There was a wash-house and one or two store-rooms. And to our joy there was a spreading oak tree with a swing hanging from it.

Near the base of the lighthouse stood a large black buoy, on a prominent place on the lawn. This was the first flashing buoy, another invention of the Stevenson family. Lit by gas, it had been moored in 1880 near Greenock. A brass plate announces that the engineer involved in the construction of the lighthouse and ancillary buildings was Robert, grandfather of the famous writer, Robert Louis Stevenson. Now, many years later, the buoy has been transferred to a site in Greenock and restored to its original colours of red, white and black.

The first thing we children did was to explore our immediate surroundings. The area outside the wall was flat and grassy on either side, the hillside rising behind. From our house, which faced south, we wandered past the engine-room down to Steadholm, a little bay with a landing slip. On the way, we stopped to admire the Round Table – a large stone mill-wheel atop a stone plinth. Guarded by two large rocks which resembled heads looking out in different diections, it became a favourite picnic spot. From the lighthouse in the other direction a path led gently down to the North Landing where there was also a slipway, which was very seldom used. We thought these were probably the original landing areas before the present arrangements. Now they were resorted to very rarely, the modern landing site being below the lighthouse compound. There was a pier for the *Torch* to off-load and take on goods and a little harbour with steps sheltered by a low wall. A tramline with a truck led to the foot of the cliff, from whence heavy goods could be winched by crane to the grounds above.

The principal keeper and his wife belonged to Greenock. Jimmy Gordon was big and bluff and impressed us hugely by his swimming prowess. We had heard that Mrs Gordon was an opera singer. It is doubtful if we knew what an opera was, but it sounded important so we knew she would be tall and flamboyant. But to our disappointment she was small and retiring and never a tra-la-la did we hear; she probably judged a Mozart aria would have been wasted on us anyway. One day a dashing young son appeared in full military regalia – swinging kilt, tartan socks, gold braid, brass buttons; mesmerising! Ernest, we learned, was a captain with the Argyll and Sutherland Highlanders and was home on leave from Malaya where he had been training troops in jungle warfare. Next day he had gone.

Some months later there was a sombre mood that even we youngsters were aware of. In February 1942 Singapore had fallen to the Japanese and for some time our neighbours were without news of their son, Ernest. Now news had come through that he was ill in a prisoner-of-war camp and they did not know whether he was dead or alive. As we were about to go out to play, Mum told us that, of course, Mr and Mrs Gordon were worried. It was bad news and we must be considerate of their concern and refrain from making a din outside their windows. We listened attentively; yes, we did understand, and off we went with our skipping ropes. It was all very mysterious. After some time our voices wafted through the window and, to her consternation, Mum picked up the drift of our latest skipping rhyme, sung lustily to a tune of our own composing:

"*One Two Three Four;*
Ernie's lost in Singapore,
S-I-N-G-A-P-O-O-R
SING-GA-PORE!"

The word 'Singapore' had a certain resonance that Flora simply could not resist! Anyway, we blamed her for the lack of good taste and poor spelling – and were forcibly settled indoors. With chamois leather dusters tied around our feet we were let loose in the lobby that ran the length of the house. We happily slid up and down until exhaustion felled us, by which time the brown linoleum was polished to a mirror glow.

Ernest Gordon later wrote about his experiences as a prisoner forced to work on the notorious 'railway of death' between Thailand and Burma. *Miracle on the River Kwai*, later made into a film, is a moving account of the courage and wonderful resilience of the human spirit in intolerable situations. After the war he studied theology and became assistant minister of Paisley Abbey. He wrote several books and went on to become dean of the chapel at Princeton University in America.

We loved Wee Cumbrae with its panoramic views. Goatfell on Arran lay directly opposite, while the sun setting over Bute traced a golden pathway over the water. In summer the bracken that covers much of the island is fresh green but, come autumn, the island is a tapestry of russet and gold against grey rock. In springtime, before the fresh fronds of bracken appear, the hillside delights with a haze of bluebells and the voice of the cuckoo makes us smile. To the south the quaint haystack mass of Ailsa Craig loomed approximately half-way between Glasgow and Belfast and so was familiarly called 'Paddy's Milestone' due to the considerable migration of Irish labourers who came to Scotland for work during the Industrial Revolution.

Steadholm Bay was a favourite spot for both adults and children. We guddled in rock-pools while the anglers among us caught the fish which, with new potatoes from the garden, made a meal fit for a king. It was a rocky shore but to the left of the slipway a small pebbly area allowed for paddling and restricted swimming. It was here that we learned to swim. Not for us the formality of lessons at the public baths! Dad stood on the edge of the long slipway with a stout walking stick extended and as we held on we were towed along. Somehow his methods worked!

The beach dipped suddenly and a few yards out surged the open sea where frolicked seals and porpoises. Dad took a keen interest in the natural world. His observant eye would spot something long before we did but he would afford us the excitement of discovering it ourselves. We were enchanted when we came across our first seal pup sunning itself on a flat rock. The mother was nowhere in sight which was unusual. We could hardly tear ourselves away from the engaging little creature with its shiny, round, fearless eyes fixed on us. The scene must have imprinted itself on Dad's mind for, years later, he would tell his grandchildren:

"Remember, never hurt a baby seal!"

Another day there was a swan resting by the water's edge, its brood of cygnets fossicking around in the shingle. At our approach mother swan signalled the alarm and as she hurried into the water her little family scrambled awkwardly on to her back. Off she glided like a well-laden Spanish galleon, leaving a perfect wake behind her. Scenes like these are never to be forgotten. Years later, when sitting my Higher English exam, I remember putting these incidents to good use in an essay entitled '*The Calm Sequestered Vale of Life*'.

But exploring had to wait as school called – and school was in Millport on Big Cumbrae. It was left to the keeper to make his own arrangements, so we lived in a rented house with Mum during term time. Friends often asked: "What's it like to live in a lighthouse?" while we wondered: "What's it like to live in an ordinary house?" We were about to find out, though it didn't feel like an ordinary house, because we knew it was temporary, nor did it have our 'stamp' on it.

That was a happy time, making new friends in school and in the pleasant little town that curved round a wide, sandy beach on which we spent many sunny hours. Cumbrae School was a primary and junior-secondary school, composed of a seven-year primary department and a three-year secondary department. Those intending a full secondary course attended Rothesay Academy on the Isle of Bute.

My earliest memories date from just before my fifth birthday, when I joined my four older sisters in school. However it came about – for rationing was still in force – we had a chocolate bar to share, its fat squares full of brilliant green peppermint cream. My share was firmly wedged against my wooden pencil-case in the outer pocket of my school-bag. As we progressed along Stuart Street, children spilled out of the various doorways until there was quite a troop advancing on the school at the top of the brae.

Wherever there were children there was a dog tagging along. That day my whole being was focused on one thing – that chocolate bar – and every few yards I stopped to check that it was still there. By the time I had hauled the bag off my back for the umpteenth time and undone the buckles, I had lagged well behind the others. And when the bell rang, *they* ran and I didn't! Minutes later, an eerie stillness hung on the air, the way it does when children's voices are cut off mid-shout. Once more off came the bag for what proved a final check. Out slipped the chocolate and my faithful four-legged friend pounced on it and turned tail, the way hangers-on do. To complete my misery, when I eventually found my way into the Infant room, there was the humiliation of the latecomer's chant. The infant-mistress hoisted me to standing position on my little round-backed chair and after a brisk: "Now then; one, two, three…" my gleeful classmates intoned the dreaded, "Lazy bones, lazy bones, lazy bones!"

Some of the older boys put round a story that a certain florid-faced old gentleman was in fact a vampire – whatever that was! I had no intention of getting near enough to find out. We infants were dismissed earlier than the older pupils so I walked home alone during the precise half-hour that Mr Vampire chose to do his shopping. At sight of him I would sprint home at a rate that would have qualified for the Olympics. Mum must have concluded that bulging eyes and gasping breath were the normal outcome of a pleasant day in class.

One afternoon she came to meet me. I skipped along, hand in hand, without a care in the world – until we rounded a corner and came face to face with Mr Vampire! Mum greeted him warmly, while self-preservation dictated that I take off like the wind, leaving her to an uncertain fate. They laughed – and I was thereafter sufficiently emboldened to wave to the ex-vampire, albeit from the other side of the street.

In no time we all had our special friends. Among them were evacuees from Glasgow, Dumbarton and elsewhere. The distinctive Glasgow accent intrigued us. These children were also away from home and we felt a kinship with them; some did not even have their mother with them, but seemed to have settled happily with strangers.

Summer or winter, there was always something of interest to see in Millport, a popular seaside resort with handsome Victorian villas lining Karnes Bay. Steamers came and went between Arran, Largs and Wemyss Bay. Kerr's coal puffer seemed to be a fixture at the pier-side. On the glorious sands we built castles with our friends, raced and dared the painted crocodile rock to grab us. This rock has been a feature of the beach since 1913, when a local resident with paint and imagination enhanced the resemblance to a rather genial crocodile.

At one time the sea around Millport was reckoned to be one of the richest marine habitats in Europe. However, by the early 1950's there was a noticeable decline of life in the rock pools so beloved of children and seabirds. The Marine Biological Station, which has ties with London University, was established on the island in 1897 at the instigation of the great naturalist, David Robertson, who spent over thirty years studying the sea life around the island – after retiring from his crockery business! His enthusiasm infected his wife and she became a world expert in her own right. The laboratory was closed in October 2013 and ownership transferred to the Field Studies Council, with funding for a comprehensive programme of development and refurbishment.

The Cathedral of the Isles, built in 1852, is the smallest cathedral in Europe. The graceful Gothic-style building, seating barely one hundred, stands in a peaceful garden. The interior is beautiful with stained-glass windows throwing a soft light on polished wood and patterned floor. On one wall is displayed a brass plate in memory of George Hodge and his son, William, who were drowned in 1875 when their boat capsized near Wee Cumbrae in a sudden change of weather. One of the light-keepers saw it happen and rowed out to help. With signal courage he managed to save the three remaining boys, their mother and a young servant girl.

Another place we visited with Mum was the Old Cemetery where we marvelled at the number of inscriptions recording the deaths of young children, often several in one family and in most cases due to tuberculosis, we learned. It was sobering. One inscription was of particular interest to us. James Wallace, a keeper on Little Cumbrae lighthouse, was ferrying his children home from Millport where they attended school. Due to stormy weather, they had been stranded in Millport for three weeks. An older sister was waiting anxiously on the shore. As she and keeper Angus Kerr watched helplessly (only two keepers were employed at the time) a wave engulfed the boat and all were thrown into the water. The two boys disappeared

under the waves, weighed down by their schoolbags, but
their older sister, Netta, managed to stay afloat while
their father managed to grab hold of young Jessie. On
shore the brave lighthouse keeper and the girl promptly
launched the small dinghy and managed to rescue the
father and the girls. They searched for the boys, but
in vain, and then made off for Millport as quickly as
possible. Before reaching help little Jessie had died. The
local doctor was at the pier and did all he could to save
Netta, but it was too late. The distraught father was
carried into the Royal George Hotel at the pier's head.

Their headstone reads:

> *The teachers and scholars*
> *Of Cumbrae Public School*
> *In loving memory of*
> *Netta, Alexander*
> *John and Jessie Wallace*
> *Who were accidentally drowned*
> *On the 17th March 1893*
>
> *There is a happy land*
> *Far, far away*

All on Wee Cumbrae were aware that such could happen again.

Also of interest was the grave of the Reverend James Adams, the Millport minister who, legend has it, was in the habit of praying in church for a blessing on: "Great Cumbrae, Little Cumbrae and the adjacent islands of Great Britain and Ireland." It sounds like a joke but apparently he really did! His epitaph, chosen by himself, is in verse, partly Latin and partly English. He died in 1831 and, eccentric though he was, he left generous legacies.

Things changed when I reached the grand age of six. It coincided with a CLT ruling that the lighthouse keepers' wives were no longer permitted to spend school term on the mainland with their children. For us, that meant transmission to lodgings. Our two older sisters, with others from Millport and Arran, would go to Rothesay on the island of Bute, so arrangements had to be made for three of us in Millport.

Millport's popularity as a holiday town with a great influx of visitors, mainly from Glasgow, meant that from late spring every nook and cranny was given over to them. There was not much room left for three lighthouse girls. We eventually found lodgings with a rather stern, middle-aged widow and I, especially, was permanently home-sick. Bedtime was the really low point of the day. It was excessively early, summer or winter, and as we cooried together under our thick, khaki blanket we could hear the voices of our playmates in the street below.

Our landlady must have had a softer heart than we cared to acknowledge. Most nights she came to stand at the foot of the bed to soothe us with an evening hymn. Her forte was the second paraphrase and she put her heart into it.

"O God of Bethel by whose hand
Thy people still are fed
Who through this weary pilgrimage
Hast all our fathers led ... "

There was nothing wrong with Mrs Ramsay's voice, but when the last line transposed itself into *'has stole our father's leg'* it was all too much for six-year-old flesh and blood. The mental image of Dad hobbling up the lighthouse stairs brought on another flood of tears. Hardly the stuff of dreams!

In her wisdom Mrs Ramsay decreed that Saturday mornings in winter should be spent profitably. Flora was given the tartan canvas bag and message list and dispatched to the shops. She had the good sense to prolong her shopping trip beyond all reason and, for her pains, she had a whole sixpence to spend on herself. Meantime, Joan and I were settled at the kitchen table with our rag-rug and an assortment of skirts discarded by Mrs Ramsay and her friends. We cut four-inch strips and with the aid of a hook wove them into an oblong piece of hessian. It was hard to be enthused by the drab black and grey creation that – oh, so slowly – emerged. If only our ladies had decked themselves in pinks and purples!

However our reward almost made it worthwhile. Joan was given two pence and I, quite fairly, earned half of that. Hail, rain or tempest we'd don our pixie hats and warm coats and head for the ice-cream shop. When we pooled our wages we were able to buy a threepenny ice-cream cone between us. Joan would break off the pointy bit, fill it with a dollop of ice cream and hand it to me. I duly returned it for a refill the moment it was empty. Blistered fingers forgotten, we walked and licked and talked – and kept an eye on the dog skulking at our heels.

I must have been somewhat of a trial to my stoical big sisters and I am sure they were secretly relieved the day I absconded. It was a Saturday, a fresh spring morning. Saturday was our favourite day because we could go down to the pier to watch for the lighthouse boat. There was great rivalry to see who could spot it first and eagerly we anticipated it curving round past the coal puffer, the *Saxon* (later to appear on television as the *Vital Spark* in the comedy series *Para Handy*). If Dad was at the tiller and Mum in the bow that was joy. However, on this particular day, the second assistant keeper was on duty. He was kind enough not to mind us tagging along, holding on to his big basket. Came time for him to leave and my sisters busied themselves with the ropes, helping to pull the boat close to the steps beside the pier. I saw my chance and sprackled aboard. Absolutely nothing and nobody could persuade me to budge; I sat resolutely on my hands and turned my head from the cajoling voices. At last the ropes were loosened, the engine sparked into life and, joy of joys, we were off, heading for *home*. I released one hand briefly to wave to the two small figures on the pier and my spirits soared with the wind. It turned out to be a very rough crossing, so I was doubly glad when the boat mounted the cradle at its third attempt and we were safely winched up the slipway. I scrambled to terra firma and made a dash for home. On no account would Dad get the chance to return me to my rightful abode!

Our cosy kitchen had never seemed so inviting and what a welcome! I savoured every minute of that weekend, safe in the knowledge that I could not be deported until Tuesday.

Only rarely did the boat run on other than the designated days and my truancy hardly constituted an emergency. Anyway, it didn't happen again. I suspect Dad warned the keepers to anchor outwith leaping distance, especially if a certain character was seen to be loitering with intent.

Incidentally, Dad was once asked if he had ever considered himself in real danger on the sea. He referred, perhaps among other instances, to one occasion when I was the only passenger. The weather dictated that he should take the route by the south of the island, as the east side should be safe, but a sudden gale whipped up the sea and he knew we were in peril. He said that, if I had not been with him, he would have made for the shore and scrambled for land as best he could, but he knew I would not survive so he just had to go on and face the ferocious Tan. He may, or may not, have been referring to my return on Tuesday to where I belonged. In any case, I was happily content with my stolen week-end.

Summer came, holidays and home and long, endless days of sunshine. Perhaps not quite so idyllic as memory says, but almost so!

Chapter Six
HOLIDAYS AT HOME

If storm-clouds dominated the winter months, unfailingly the month of May ushered in balmy air and tranquil seas and uninterrupted sunshine, as I recall! Maytime was bluebell time, when the island was clothed in swathes of hazy blue while the air was sweet with their perfume. For the following weeks, from the first day of our summer vacation, we were seldom indoors – the whole island was our garden and we wandered at will. I suppose caution or common sense should have dictated our boundaries, but being children we weren't brimful of either of these! Our skimpy summer dresses gave our limbs every chance of turning mahogany brown right to the tip of our toes, which never saw shoes all summer.

We learned to cycle on Wee Cumbrae, despite its lack of a road. In one of the sheds we found a lethal racing bike with neither brakes nor tyres. With the aid of a hearty push the intrepid cyclist took off, pedalling furiously over the grass and down a slope, to fall gracefully off – the alternative to careering over the cliff. That is when glycerine-and-Epsom-Salts poultices came into their own. With knee bandaged, off we'd go with Dad's invariable: "Now go and see if you can do the same to the other one!" ringing in our ears. This puzzled us but, like good children, we were quick to obey!

Those halcyon days were superbly long. Holidaymakers took full advantage of them to book a boat-trip from Millport to view our lighthouse. The *Sunbeam*, packed with its cheery load, sat so low in the water that its passengers seemed to us to be individually bouncing along on the crest of the tippy waves! Some of the visitors made for Steadholm, perhaps stopping to have a look at the engine room topped by its giant horn, or to sit on the wooden bench halfway along the path, while others opted for a trip up the tower.

In summer any period of drought necessitated an expedition to the water tank to check the water level. Built into the hillside, it was little more than 300 yards beyond the perimeter wall, but we felt as if we were tackling the Himalayas. We younger ones clamoured to carry the gear required for the operation so, to satisfy our Sherpa instincts, the stirrup pump was dismantled and shared out. As a final touch we sometimes brought a simple picnic and after our expedition we came back full of news and views, as if we had been to the other side of the world. If the water level was precariously low the old water pump came into use. Standing among the bracken, it looked rather like a grand old lady with bell-shaped hat and arms akimbo. We took turns at pumping the handle up and down and were surprised when the clear water really flowed. Of course we had now to be sparing of water, a salutary lesson. We children spent a great deal of time playing in the sea or rock pools, so baths were not a priority.

On boat days it was such a pleasure to be out on the sea that one could wish the journey never to end. The boat chugged along at half-speed, close to the shore where the greenery was reflected in the pale blue calm while the nesting birds looked impassively down at us as we admired them. And occasionally, for the joy of it, the boat would take the long way to Millport round the south of the island for a close look at the cliffs and caves there. Seagulls nested in abundance in mid-spring. There was a timelessness about their plaintive mewing as they circled their territory, dipping and rising, diving and wheeling. All kinds of sea birds inhabited the nooks and crannies in the cliffs to the southwest – cormorants, guillemots, gannets, fulmars and black-headed gulls as well as common gulls. On the slippery rocks below, colonies of shag stood, hunch-backed, drying their greenish-black wings and calling to one another in their distinctive rasping tones. There could be seen the King's Cave where Robert the Bruce met a famous spider. The entrance to the Monks' Cave was a narrow cleft in the rock but the large cavern reached back a considerable distance. It was said that on the ledges lining the walls the monks of old made their beds.

Such weather tempted the ladies to join the shopping trips to Millport. In those days no self-respecting woman went to town without a hat. So, boat or no boat, the lighthouse keepers' wives dressed up when they crossed to the mainland. One sunny morning the wife of one of the keepers made her appearance dressed as for a banquet – as was appropriate, for she was indeed to attend a function in Millport. We gazed admiringly at her up-to-the-minute midi-length brown dress and fetching hat. On the return trip in late afternoon, a mischievous wind drenched the boat with spray and our lady shrank into the farthest corner under the hood. Her crepe dress shrank too and, when she clambered off the boat, she was sporting a mini-dress decades ahead of fashion. If we had gaped in the morning we had twice as much – or half as much – to stare at now. Our gallant keepers appeared to notice nothing amiss but we, lacking all finesse, enjoyed her chagrin hugely.

One happy day Mum came home from Millport looking pleased and, with an innocent air, mentioned casually that she had bought a piano 'for a song' at a sale, and that it was to be picked up at our convenience. "*Convenience!*" exploded Dad. "How did she think they were to get a hulk like that on to the boat, never mind...etcetera, etcetera.....?" Mum acted deaf. But manage it they did, with considerable good-humoured, not to say witty, grumbling. The whole community (except Mum) turned out to watch as it was hauled from the railway up the cliff and, with many a heave and shove, deposited in our sitting-room. It was a beautiful piece of furniture. No wonder she could not resist it with its polished silky walnut and a fretwork front lined with primrose yellow silk.

In the absence of a grand piano Flora had made do with our substantial chest of drawers. The five drawers were pulled out to graduated levels and on these she clattered and banged like a true virtuoso, hand flourishes and all. Joan and I were cajoled into accompanying her in song, the frequent mismatch between vocalists and pianist leading us to experience the rough edge of her temperamental tongue. With a curt nod Madame would then give the opening bar, *crash, bang, clatter-ty bang* and when we simultaneously burst into different songs it was more than our *prima donna* could tolerate. So the piano was welcomed with excited enthusiasm.

During the war years, three English naval gentlemen were stationed on Wee Cumbrae. There was a slogan 'careless talk costs lives' so, probably for that reason, we children were not enlightened as to why they had come to the island. They divided their time between the radio room and a little look-out post about 200 yards north of the lighthouse, where they lived in tents and kept themselves largely to themselves.

One of these men, Trevor, was a larger than life character. In his spare time he gathered together bits and pieces of corrugated iron, wood and nails. We trotted along beside him as he wheeled load after load towards the north landing. We were mystified and he kept us guessing! At a chosen spot against a rock face he constructed a bolt-hole for himself. Once it was complete with roof, door and tiny window he hung out a sign which proudly swung and creaked in the breeze, proclaiming 'the Squeeze Inn' ready for occupation. The den was cosily furnished with two chairs, a table and a box fire. To us it was the proverbial fairy-tale cottage, the home of the three little pigs! When autumn evenings drew in and the first wisps of smoke curled from its chimney, it looked most inviting and the lighthouse keepers occasionally gravitated towards the peaceful little retreat. We, on the other hand, knowing instinctively that it was a private haven, never even dreamt of intruding.

We were more than content with a very special property of our own. It was our first ever doll's house. In the evenings the three Navy men had spent long hours making it and, to our total surprise, we received it on Christmas morning. It was substantial and beautifully furnished with all sorts of miniatures. Its yellow and red paintwork was immaculate and everything inside worked to perfection. Over the years we enjoyed renewing bedspreads, curtains and carpets when we felt it was time for a change. I don't suppose these kind men ever realised just how much pleasure their gift would give.

The war had created a demand for seaweed from which a variety of commodities could be made so, on balmy summer evenings, the menfolk set to work and we also did our bit. There seemed to be an endless amount of it and at low tide we gathered and sang on the rocks at Steadholm as we filled the big hessian bags. Our repertoire was a wide one; *Oh Rowan Tree*, *The Mountains of Mourne* that sweep down to the sea; *Skye Boat Song* and:

> *"Westering home with a song in the air*
> *Light in the eye and it's goodbye to care;*
> *Laughter o'love and a welcoming there;*
> *Isle of my heart, my own one."*

Happy and hungry we made for home and supper under a sunset sky. Darkness fell and the stars came out. The silence of peace descended.

Next day the heavy bags, picked up at Steadholm slipway, weighed down the boat as it set off for Millport. Bladderwrack was used for soap-making and much more. We sent dark curly carrageen too, but some we kept for ourselves. Washed and left under the sun for days it bleached white and dried. A few fronds boiled in milk with a touch of sugar made a delicious set dessert.

We were now in the principal's house, connected to the lighthouse by a long corridor or lobby. A heavy oak door led into the radio room at the foot of the lighthouse tower. While we were young we were not allowed through that door unaccompanied. That area belonged to the men and we knew our place! Directly through that door was the radio room in which was valuable equipment. The calibration charts mystified us. We watched as the needle progressed along the paper, leaving a series of squiggly lines which meant nothing to us, however much we gazed.

There also was the transmitter set, which the keepers used for communicating with the outside world. There was no telephone on the island. Every two hours, at two o'clock, four o'clock and so on, there was a slot of time for Cumbrae and Toward lighthouses to get in touch, if both remembered – which they usually did, though there were times when one or the other would forget, or remember just too late. Before transmitting a message the keeper would pinpoint his location in clear precise tones: "Charlie, Uncle, Michael, Brian, Roger, Alec, Easy." One of the keepers greatly enhanced it with his soft Isle of Skye accent and we appropriated it for our repertoire of skipping rhymes. Our playmates could not make head or tail of it and teachers found it amusing.

We loved, as a rare treat, to accompany Dad up to the light-room. The powerful beam sweeping over the sea gave the impression that the source of it was a huge blinding light inside the tower. Not so – the light in the centre of the large circular platform had in fact much the same power as would have lit a large drawing-room of those times. The light projection was due entirely to the magnifying power of heavy lenses or mirrors. We were amazed to find that a soft push was enough to set the huge platform rotating at a stately, deliberate pace.

The machinery fascinated us. We could only compare it to the old grandfather clock in our lobby. The large weight that regulated the machinery took about half an hour to descend to the bottom when a satisfactory 'clunk' announced that it was time to rewind. We took turns at helping turn the handle and, task completed, congratulated ourselves on keeping the entire sea-faring fraternity safe for another night.

The three lighthouses had the same basic mechanism with minor differences. For instance, in the case of both Cloch and Toward the platform rotated on a bath of mercury while Cumbrae's was set on metal rollers. Cloch and Toward each had a clear-weather range of 14 miles while Cumbrae's light could be seen 16 miles off. While Cloch and Cumbrae used lenses, with vaporised paraffin for the light, Toward used acetylene gas and concave mirrors. It is the positioning of the lenses or mirrors on the platform combined with the speed at which the platform revolves that determines the pattern of flashes.

The Cumbrae light had thick curving prisms which in daylight, and especially in sunlight, reflected a waltz of rainbow colours that linger in memory. Mirrors and reflectors were kept scrupulously clean and gleaming and blinds were lowered during daylight hours. We felt a sense of wonder at the simplicity and precision of it all – that small light, so effective and yet a child could understand it – almost manage it!

The final treat was to step outside on to the balcony which was protected by a stout rail. We really did feel on top of the world as we chased one another round and round. If it was dark that was even better! We watched the light travel along the hill-top – *flash, flash*, pause, *flash, flash* – to land's end and take off into the darkness. One afternoon, from our vantage point, we watched a splendid aircraft-carrier as it exercised right opposite the lighthouse, the sailors bustling about on deck. We passed the binoculars round and Dad mounted his powerful telescope. Gliding down the river an aeroplane came in close to make a perfect landing, and we watched as the crew moved into position to make room for the others that followed in swift succession.

The arrival of the pilot boat was exciting. It lay off the island of Bute in readiness to escort ships bound for the busy ports of Greenock, Port Glasgow or the docks of Glasgow itself. The channel between Little Cumbrae and the southern tip of Bute is just over a mile wide, so the large ships took the pilot on board to guide them. Ships heading on up to Glasgow might have to wait at the 'Tail o' the Bank' off Greenock for a few hours for high water before being able to progress up the river, which has a narrow, buoyed channel between sandbanks, and for this the local knowledge of a Clyde Navigation Trust river pilot was a necessity. To us it was a David and Goliath scenario, with the sturdy little boat taking control of one of the giant liners of the Cunard fleet, or a heavily laden freighter.

The annual inspection day came round each spring. It was a pleasant outing for the Clyde Lighthouse Trustees and, in its own way, a highlight for us. For the keepers and their wives – even their children – it was the culmination of weeks of effort to achieve the highest gleam and polish, inside and out. Buildings, lawns and paths were in perfect trim. The kitchen range, always well black-leaded, glowed as never before. Bedrooms had an unnerving clutter-free, never-been-occupied air and books stood upright on their shelves. Even the flowers on the sideboard stood to attention. Everyone was dressed as for a royal visit. It never occurred to us that the purpose of the visitors might be to see what improvements were required in the service both for sea-farers and keepers. We basely suspected that the formality was an excuse for the gentlemen to have a nice day out and equally for keepers and wives to rally the workforce to maximum effort. It certainly succeeded in that!

On the dot of ten o'clock on the appointed day the *Torch* hove into view with a 'Greetings to you all!' hoot of the horn. Its crew was made up mainly of men from the Outer Isles and Dad was always glad to have a conversation with them in his native Gaelic. As the boat neared Little Cumbrae the keepers lined up, immaculate in full uniform, the principal keeper first in line, followed by the first assistant while the second assistant took up the rear. Mr Watson, the clerk of works, introduced everyone, there were handshakes all round and the visiting party was escorted to the lighthouse premises. There was much pomp and circumstance. Children were considered too much of a risk in such august company and were dispatched to Steadholm Bay.

When a good time had been had by all, the visitors took their leave with hearty handshakes and thanks. With a farewell blast from its horn, the *Torch* was off and an answering call from our foghorn signalled the end of a successful day. We had all done our bit, so there were mutual congratulations and a general glow of satisfaction in a test safely passed. There were, of course, tales of near disasters – how one of the dignitaries had made to open the big walk-in cupboard at the foot of the stairs and the keeper had tactfully indicated that perhaps he had better not. The gentleman gave an understanding nod and desisted. Another had unthinkingly opened it and all were agreed that he deserved the avalanche that descended on his head!

Were inspections perhaps triggered, we wondered, by a certain contravention of lighthouse regulations away back in the 1850's? The trustees had got wind that the keepers were making a little extra income by letting out their houses to summer visitors while they and their families moved into the outhouses. A keeper at Cloch lighthouse even had a permanent lodger! Worse still, they discovered that the keepers were leaving the light unattended for hours as they frittered away their time: "*no doubt playing Nap round a brazier in the basement*." Thereafter the trustees made a determined effort to keep an eye on these outposts.

The CLT updated the houses regularly. We totally failed to see any connection between the arrival of wallpaper books and the inspection as we assiduously studied them and gave Mum our individual advice. Like the other women she sensibly made her own decision and soon the workmen arrived. Workmen (our all-inclusive word for painters, decorators, joiners, engineers etc) were usually picked up on a Monday and invariably arrived full of good cheer as if on holiday. And off they would go on Friday equally full of good cheer at the prospect of a weekend at home!

Early one evening we looked up and straggling down the path came a little group of strangers! Not all strangers – Mrs Urquhart from the farm side we knew. Her husband was the gamekeeper on the island. One of the former owners had introduced rabbits to the island so that his guests might enjoy some shooting and now they burrowed everywhere. Deer had once roamed the island, too, but in our time it was sheep that were pastured there, wandering freely and helping to keep the bracken in check. So we often came across jovial Mr Urquhart in our wanderings.

Mrs Fletcher, the wife of the gardener at the manor, introduced her daughter and her four granddaughters – Gladys, Olive, Rose, and Violet. The little family had been living in Paris but with the fall of France they had decided to come back to Britain and were staying meantime with Mrs Fletcher. Their father had been in charge of gardens in Paris and was now on the mainland making arrangements for their future. Meanwhile it was good to have them pop over on occasion. When school resumed Violet shared lodgings with my older sisters in Rothesay, for summer could not last for ever and, as the months rolled round, winter came with its trials and joys.

If the howling wind and cold feet failed to keep us awake the wailing foghorn did its best. Strangely enough, after a while the familiar 'mooing' sound could have quite a soporific effect. It was familiar and comforting on dark, sometimes wild nights. In fact, if the foghorn had been blowing for perhaps 20 hours, it merged into the background and it often happened that we would suddenly hear, as it were, silence and think: "Oh, it's stopped!" only to learn that it had stopped 'about half an hour ago'. Or we'd become aware of a change of rhythm, a slowing in the up-and-down vibration, winding down into a silence that we felt rather than heard.

Winter had its joys. To look out over the balustrade at the foot of the tower in a storm and wonder at the waves hurling themselves against the rock-face, as the wind tore at our hair and we had to shout to outdo the gale was exhilarating. Equally, when the wind got up and the boat had to land at the farm side, the walk home with the wind strong in our faces and the sea foaming ahead was a thrilling experience, as we felt the tremendous power of nature. And it made sitting in a cosy room with a roaring fire and a book doubly enjoyable.

The CLT thoughtfully provided a certain amount of literature for their keepers. The daily newspapers the *Glasgow Herald* and the *Daily Express* were delivered by post. Then there was the *Illustrated London News* and the sailors' religious periodical, *Living Links*, which carried some wonderful and thought-provoking articles. There were also full bound sets of *Sunday at Home*, *Life and Work*, *Good Words*, *Family Treasury*, *Christian Treasury* and perhaps other titles. The keepers were also supplied with the usual First Aid box and a medical book that covered every ailment from fainting to cholera. Added to that was an intriguing variety of tomes, some very old, which had come from Mum's childhood home.

A special favourite among our books was John Bunyan's *Pilgrim's Progress*. Our copy of Bunyan's works was large and ornate with a brass clasp to close it. It was so heavy that the best way to tackle it was to place it on our sturdy living-room table and kneel on a chair alongside it. The sepia illustrations were protected by a sheet of tissue paper. We liked to first view the picture through the film of paper in anticipation of the sharper image; it gave some meaning to 'seeing through a glass darkly'. To us the Slough of Despond was the marshy area we passed on the way to the other side of the island. Giant Despair's Castle was Cumbrae's own castle and without doubt the Valley of Humiliation was just below the Hill Difficulty to the north of the old tower! My favourite illustration was a beautiful depiction of Christian being welcomed by the Shining Ones. I immediately related them to our new friends whose flower names added to their ethereal quality and whenever they appeared at the brow of the hill I fancied I could see their shimmering wings. How it vexed my spirit that their parents had not called the oldest 'Gladiola', instead of 'Gladys' – merely hinting at the beautiful flowers in our sundial garden.

Sundays on the island were special, a rest from the activities of the week. Even the gardens were left in peace and no washing flapped on lines. Whatever the weather there was a quiet calm that could be felt. Once we had a young friend holidaying with us and Johnny remarked on it, too: "It's funny, I thought Sabbath would be the same as other days, because there's no church or anything to make it different, but it is. I don't know what it is – it's as if it's made of different stuff!" We knew what he meant.

Not surprisingly many of our favourite stories were connected with the sea. Our heroine was the young Grace Darling of the Longstone lighthouse on the lonely Farne Islands in the north of England. In 1838 William Darling, keeper of the light, was assisted by his 22-year-old daughter. We never tired of hearing how Grace helped her father to row their small, flat-bottomed boat through mountainous seas, valiantly going to the aid of nine survivors from the *Forfarshire*, a stricken passenger steamer carrying 63 people from Hull to Dundee. The small rescue boat could not hold all nine people so Grace and her father repeated the half-mile trip to Big Harcar Rock, on which the ship had foundered, and to which the survivors were desperately clinging. They successfully rescued all nine and cared for them in the lighthouse for two days until the storm abated. Grace became internationally famous and hundreds of people made trips to the Farne Islands to view the scene of the rescue. Sadly, Grace died four years after her heroic deed.

Strangely, but understandably, among the many lighthouse regulations was one that stated that lighthouse keepers must: 'take notice of a wreck, report it and log it', but they must not get involved in it. Their place of duty was strictly by the light. It was imperative that at all times at least one keeper should remain on the lighthouse premises. '*The lighthouse keeper on duty shall at his peril remain on guard 'til he is relieved by the light keeper in person who has the next watch.'*

Another story that gripped us was the unsolved mystery of the three lighthouse keepers who, in December 1900, disappeared without trace from the far-flung Flannan Light, a lonely outpost 17 miles west of the Hebridean Isle of Lewis. At the time it stirred the imagination of the whole nation and gave rise to much wild speculation. Had a fight broken out among the keepers and had they tumbled into the sea? Had pirates abducted them? Or extraterrestrial aliens? Had six weeks cooped up together driven one of them mad? Wilfred Gibson's atmospheric poem talks of an ancient curse that had been put on the island and suggests that the three keepers had been turned into gaunt, black, raven-like birds.

A likely explanation came from the lighthouse superintendent whom the Northern Lighthouse Board commissioned to conduct an investigation. He came to the conclusion that the men had probably been down on the landing stage, perhaps securing some equipment, when an exceptionally large freak wave had swept them off the rock. The lighthouse had been built only the previous year and the power of wind, sea and tide in certain varied conditions was, as yet, not fully known. Keepers discovered that when wind and sea are in opposition, a huge column of water smashing into particular gullies in the rock can be thrown eighty feet into the air and come crashing down on the path beneath. Whatever the explanation, the strange happening left lighthouse keepers distinctly nervous about taking up duty on that remote, sea-beaten rock.

We had boundless admiration for those intrepid and resourceful men who manned the lonely rock stations around our coasts and were glad that we were restricted to our three stations.

Chapter Seven
WHO GO TO THE SEA IN SHIPS

I must go down to the seas again,
for the call of the running tide
Is a wild call and a clear call
that may not be denied;
And all I ask is a windy day
with the white clouds flying,
And the flung spray and the blown
spume, and the seagulls flying.

The sound of the sea can be disturbing to those who have no kinship with it but it was music in our ears. We could empathise with John Masefield's nostalgic lines. However, there were times when the 'flung spray and the blown spume' did give cause for concern, for fear and sometimes even resulted in tragedy.

Tides and boats were a central part of life on Wee Cumbrae. The lighthouse motor-boat rested on a cradle in the boatshed, from whence the cradle ran down the slipway into the sea and the boat floated off with a bounce. The cradle was then retracted. The sea had to be above a certain minimum depth for the launch and retrieval to be safely accomplished, so trips had to be co-ordinated with the tide. This was usually no problem, but if a storm was brewing and prudence indicated an immediate return to the island the tide might dictate delay for an hour – or two – which could make for difficulties.

On its return, the boat had to be steered with precision on to the cradle sitting in the water. When settled into position the boatman signalled to the keeper at the winch and the cradle was pulled up to dry land. If the steersman failed to get the boat into the exact position, he would retreat and try again. He might even have to make three attempts, depending on a number of circumstances. In stormy weather this manoeuvre was especially tricky. The boat might be in perfect position on the cradle and just as it was settling down and before the winchman could act, in a trice the swell or a powerful wave might lift it and plonk it down awry or pull it away altogether. It was all a matter of judgement, timing and decision on the part of the two men – and a third might be ready with boathook to help as necessary. Sometimes it was too hazardous to think of having a second try and the cradle would be taken up sufficiently to allow passengers to get out; or they might have to climb the iron ladder at the side of the pier. The boat would then be tied in the middle of the heaving harbour till the weather calmed.

Ordinarily, passengers would embark and alight at the little jetty that formed the harbour wall – though children usually liked to experience the run down the slipway and the splash into the water – but in really difficult circumstances the priority was safety. We children gauged just how nerve-wracking a journey was likely to prove by how soon the boatman reached for the rope to pull up the canvas hood protecting the bow. That was the signal to hang on tightly as each wave slapped the hood and he ducked to avoid the flung spume.

One year a mad March wind prolonged our Easter holiday by five days. However, a new day dawned to reveal a wan sun and a mild, playful breeze and we resigned ourselves to returning to our desks. But Dad could read the sky and the sea better than we could. Ominous clouds were gathering in the west and the wind's playfulness was threatening to get out of hand. Dad reckoned that the Tan, the stretch of water between the Cumbraes, where two strong currents converge, might be too much of a hazard for a small boat laden with five children and the accoutrements required for a whole school term.

On this occasion we were delighted to be excused school for yet another day. Dad, on his own, was to make a quick dash to the mainland. Perhaps essential supplies were running low. There was a following wind so his crossing went well, but no sooner had he left Millport on the return journey than the wind whipped the sea into a turmoil. We could see the boat in the distance. It was making heavy weather of it and the two keepers were grimfaced as they hurried to the shore in preparation for its arrival. The cradle was winched into position and we children were sternly warned to keep well back from the action. The wind tugged at us as we and cousin Donald, who was agog to see how the operation worked, huddled together in the doorway of the boat shed.

We kept our eyes fixed on Skart rock and at last the sturdy little boat appeared round the point. Like an untamed colt it bucked and tossed amid the waves while Dad wrestled with the tiller. One keeper, thigh-deep in water, hung on tenaciously to the side of the iron cradle, his boat-hook at the ready. The other keeper, of course, had to stay firmly by the winch, to act quickly when the boat mounted the cradle. In a storm like this that was a really tricky manoeuvre. If the boat missed the cradle it was liable to be dashed against the rocks at the entrance to the harbour. Once, twice, thrice Dad tried to mount the cradle as we watched anxiously. At each failed attempt, he had to take a sweep out into the treacherous open sea and try again. All this time he had his hand cupped round his mouth as though calling to us. To our frustration, the sound was snatched away by the voracious wind.

At last we caught the words: "Oil! Oil!" We jumped aside as the keeper by the cradle left his place and dashed up to the boat shed to grab a large can of oil. With difficulty, he slithered down the slipway as far as he dared. Grappling the lid from the can he tipped its contents into the sea around the cradle. An almost immediate calm ensued and Dad took his chance to mount the cradle. The winchman deftly pulled cradle, with boat and boatman, to safety. The wind made short work of dispersing the oil and in a moment the sea reverted to its former fury. All this time we had waited in anxious silence, well aware of the drama being played out before us. Now we erupted in a torrent of chatter. Talk about pouring oil on troubled waters!

It's all we could talk about! Dad was more subdued. He knew only too well what could have happened.

Things did not go so well later in the year. On Christmas Eve our boat prepared to make the crossing to Millport. Since a storm was brewing, it was decreed that only the keeper on duty, Mr MacQueen from the Isle of Skye, was to go that morning – women and children were banned. Armed with outsize shopping basket and three extra-long shopping lists, the keeper manned the boat down the slipway, off the cradle and away out into the growling sea. Pre-Christmas excitement was in the air, but more was to come!

Mid-day came and went. The old grandfather clock in the lobby struck one, two, three, four o'clock. Darkness began to gather and still the boat did not return. My father made countless sorties to the look-out at North Landing, three of us padding along behind him. Each time we could sense his growing agitation and we kept suitably quiet as he scanned the turbulent sea with his binoculars. We had only to look at the troubled faces of the adults to know that something was badly wrong.

Darkness proper came down, the wind muttered ominously. While the other keeper was up in the tower tending the light, Dad made yet another expedition to the North Landing, the three of us at his heels. Yet again he peered into the gloom, which by now was lit up intermittently by the sweep of the light. We heard his sharp intake of breath and, when we followed his gaze, we made out the figure of the missing keeper stumbling over the slippery boulders. We were summarily despatched homewards and our half-relieved Dad made off to meet the wanderer. The following week, when the storm abated, the badly-damaged boat was salvaged but mail, shopping, the lot, were lost for good. It transpired that the boat had been swamped by a huge wave, but providentially the keeper had been hugging the shoreline and, being a very strong swimmer, he was able to save himself. So we had a leaner festive season than usual, which did us no harm!

At the foot of the tower was the look-out, with a balustrade on which we could lay our elbows and gaze out over the Firth. With ships coming and going – puffers, liners, trawlers, battleships, destroyers, mine-sweepers, frigates and giant aircraft-carriers – there was constant activity. Convoys of anything up to forty ships sailed south escorted by one, perhaps two fighting ships or an aircraft-carrier, while incoming ships were met by the busy little pilot boats. Dredging went on constantly.

Out there, just two years into the war, the cargo ship SS *Rockpool* was making good speed after daring the hazards of the Atlantic and was safe in home waters

– or so thought the crew as they sailed into the Firth.
Then, so near home, the ship somehow landed with a
juddering jolt on the rocks at the south of Wee Cumbrae
and effectively came to a sorry end. But not quite. So
desperate was the need for ships that the hull was rescued
and, rebuilt, she gallantly fought on to the end of the war.

On 27th March 1943 Dad was in the tower
preparing for lighting up. He remembered it as a sunny
afternoon, with a bit of a haze in the far distance,
typical of the days in late spring. About five miles to
the south of Little Cumbrae, between Ardrossan on
the Ayrshire coast and the island of Arran, a British
aircraft carrier, the *Dasher*, was engaged, among
others, in exercises. All day long aeroplanes had been
landing and manoeuvring into position on the ships
while others practised taking off. Now Flora and Dad
were on the balcony, leaning on the rail. Dad's telescope
allowed them to see the movement on deck in detail
and they lingered for some time.

As they turned to step inside there was a loud
explosion and a brilliant flash, followed by dense black
smoke rising hundreds of feet into the air. With a second
explosion and whoosh the sea all around became a
mass of flames as oil gushed from the stricken vessel.

Hundreds of men were swimming in the water,
frantically trying to get away from the inferno while
ships in the vicinity sped to their aid. Dad and Flora

had witnessed what was probably the most serious disaster in Clyde history. As she wrote years later, "Suddenly, when one of the planes was landing, the huge explosion took place. Before our astonished eyes, and in a matter of minutes, the ship had gone." Her bow pointing dramatically skyward, she slid into a deep, dark pit. My sister remembered how shaken and troubled Dad was, though he said little about it.

Much later the full impact of the disaster was brought to light. The explosion had occurred at 4.40 pm and eight minutes later the ship had disappeared. Out of a crew of 528, as many as 379 had perished. A poignant fact has been recounted – at 4.40pm Captain L A K Boswell had announced over the ship's tannoy that shore leave was being granted on arrival at Greenock, with an estimated arrival time of 6pm. The off-duty crew was below decks, preparing for a night ashore.

Speculation as to the cause of the disaster was fuelled by the immediate clamp-down of discussion or publication of the event. The local press were ordered to make no reference to the tragedy and survivors were told not to speak about it. The *Dasher*, a US-built merchant ship, had, a year previously, been converted for use by the Royal Navy in protecting transatlantic convoys. It had been beset by problems and, on the day of the disaster, had turned back from a mission because of a technical fault. Various explanations for the disaster were put forward; a torpedo from a German U-boat, aviation fluid on board igniting, diesel igniting, a mine previously dropped by a plane and several others. Officially the explosion was attributed to the ignition of aviation fuel vapour. Another explanation given by the Ministry of Defence was a plane crashing while attempting to land.

Many of the bodies were washed up on the shore at Ardrossan and are buried in the cemetery there. On 27th March 1993, a ceremony took place in the town of Ardrossan and later a memorial stone and plaque were unveiled in tribute to HMS *Dasher* and her crew. My sister Flora and her husband were privileged to attend the dedication service, 50 years after the event. Only recently I was interested to meet a lady in Lochcarron whose 18-year-old twin brother had perished in the disaster. It was moving to sit with her and have a word picture of the brother who sadly perished on the cusp of manhood and whom she so much missed.

Most memorable was the night Mum came to waken us, long after we were in bed. It was just after midnight. In conspiratorial whispers she urged us to slip on our coats and follow her. Outside, round the corner we hurried to the lookout where everyone was gathered. We shivered momentarily in the cold air and thrilled to the sight of a velvet sky bejewelled with stars. We could hear the distant throb of an engine, a familiar sound which scarcely merited the atmosphere of suppressed excitement, but no explanation was forthcoming.

Then, like a grande dame making her entrance, she swept into view – the magnificent liner, RMS *Queen Elizabeth*, the largest ship in the world at that time and predecessor to the recently decommissioned QE2 and the current Cunard liner, *Queen Elizabeth*. Her two large funnels were floodlit and her decks and rigging a feast of fairy lights. Straight out of the pages of a child's fantasy! The friendly captain sounded the ship's horn in greeting and the courtesy was returned on our foghorn. Having been engaged on troopship duties since her launch in 1940, she had just completed her post-war refurbishment as a passenger liner at Greenock and was resplendent in her new Cunard livery. In stark contrast to the blackout of the war years, now past, this spectacle seemed to speak of a new beginning of triumph and hope.

On a sunny autumn afternoon the famous HMS *Vanguard*, the largest battleship in the Royal Navy, newly commissioned, came coursing down the river bent on an important mission. We did not know it at the time, but it was on the way to pick up the Royal Family for a tour to South Africa, their first tour abroad since the war ended. It thundered past so quickly that we hardly had time to appreciate it, but we waited expectantly for the powerful wash that we knew would come in its wake. Huge waves rolled in, reaching parts of the shore where water had never been, slapping the cliff face and curling back on themselves in a welter of foam. When the powerful battleship was just a speck on the horizon, the sea slowly ceased its fretting and settled down in an uneasy calm.

VE Day on 8th May 1945 had marked the end of the war, but we scarcely noticed it as we were in school in Millport. There were doubtless celebrations but they passed us by. And there were those who scarcely felt in celebratory mood.

Chapter Eight

LONG, LONG AGO

From the hilltop above the lighthouse the path meandered unevenly across the hill with a track leading off to the right, while farther along another climbed up to the sturdy Old Tower off to the left on its own hill. We marvelled at the strength that kept it there exposed to centuries of fiercest wind and rain. At that time there was nothing to indicate its history, but later a plate was fixed above the doorway:

1756-1956

CLYDE LIGHTHOUSES TRUST

This tower is the original Cumbrae Light House.
It first gave out light to assist mariners on 8th
December 1757 following on the passing of
the Cumray Lighthouse Act on 15th April 1756
Ostendimus Litora Flammis

That was a favourite spot for a day's outing. When friends came to stay, and at other times, we often packed a picnic and when Dad's watch was over he would usually join us. We gathered sticks for a fire and brewed up strong tea in an old black kettle. While the grown-ups sat, backs to the tower, we played in and out and round about and counted the protruding stones spiralling up inside the tower, the cinders of the coal used two hundred years before digging into the soles of our bare feet. We were used to the sunshine and beauty all around us, but we still felt a glow of satisfaction at the obvious appreciation of our visitors. Our Aunt Chrissie used to declare that the stillness was 'calming to the spirit' – and that despite the presence of eight high-spirited children!

At this peaceful away-from-it-all spot the mind was drawn back to those early keepers, as it is now. Did they admire this view too?

Our little island was a place apart, rich in marine, plant and bird life and up there was a birds' playground.

It is reckoned that there are well over 50 species to be seen at various times of the year. Migratory birds found the island convenient as a staging post. The Arctic tern made it a stopover on its annual flight to the Antarctic and back – a round trip of over 22,000 miles. There were the familiar thrush, chaffinch, blackbird, magpie and the friendly robin guarding its own little patch of the island; the skylark, too, and how we welcomed the first call of the cuckoo! The swift, lapwing, ring-ousel visited and last but not least a tiny budgie! One afternoon I looked out of the window and there it was feeding on the lawn, to the annoyance of our local sparrows! It was glad to be rescued and happily settled in our own budgie's cage, bullying him shamelessly! So 'ch-ee-ee-ky wee Joey', under Dad's coaching, learned to say his name perfectly.

The mile-and-a-half walk over the hill to visit the people on the eastern side of the island made for a very pleasant outing and visitors were assured of a warm welcome. One sunny afternoon Mum gathered a few things together and she and a Millport friend, Jean, set off for the farm with some of us following on behind. On the way we met gamekeeper Mr Urquhart, hearty and affable, in tweed plus-fours with signature fore-and-aft firmly on head. He warmly invited us to tell his good lady to 'get the kettle on and I'll soon be in to join you all!'

Just before the descent to the houses, it was tempting to rest for a moment on an outcrop of rock known as Parker's Seat, to take in the view across to the Ayrshire coast from Largs to Ardrossan some miles to the south. The path twisted down through bracken and heather till suddenly there below was the Manor House, with cottages and a cluster of small buildings set among lawns and well-tended gardens.

Off-shore lies a small tidal island, Allimturrail, 'the isle of the noble 's tower' which can be visited on foot at low tide. While Mrs Urquhart dutifully got the kettle on, we went over to the islet. The castle there had once been surrounded by a moat and drawbridge. The rectangular tower had been restored to a certain extent by Evelyn Parker, who acquired Little Cumbrae in 1913. Built of local stone, the walls, six feet thick, have narrow slits and square openings – presumably for defensive purposes as well as for light. There is decorative stonework around the top as befits what was once a royal residence. Entry is by an outside stairway, which leads up to the first floor. Inside, from the main floor a stone stairway leads up through two storeys to the flat rooftop and, likewise, stairs lead down to the dungeon. It stirred the imagination to stand in a building with links to days long gone, dating back it may be to the 13th century; days when kitchen-maids, cooks, armour-clad warriors, boatmen and all and sundry mingled, each with his special responsibility.

clear view of Wee Cumbrae, with the sturdy old tower on the skyline.
his was the original Cumbrae lighthouse, which first gave out light in 1757.

The lighthouse at Toward Point stands out against the Cowal hills in Argyllshire.

Toward Point first shone its light in 1812, just as
Napoleon was embarking on his Russian campaign.

Mum and me (left), relaxing on the doorstep
at Cumbrae Lighthouse in 1958.

Looking out over the view that Johan Wodrow would have seen as she watched for a glimpse of the ship bearing her fiancé.

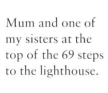

Mum and one of my sisters at the top of the 69 steps to the lighthouse.

The boat approaches the cradle at low tide. A keeper stands by on the pier to help pull her in with the boathook.

The children aboard the boat as she is made fast on the cradle.

The large black buoy near the base of the lighthouse was the first flashing buoy, another invention of the Stevenson family.

Members of our extended lighthouse 'family' including Mrs Sinclair (Archie's wife), Mum and Dad, me and my sister Flora.

The Round Table on Cumbrae, with Mum enjoying a seat.

The memorial at Ardrossan to the men lost when HMS *Dasher* sank in 1943. The tragedy was witnessed by Dad and my sister Flora.

The dungeons fascinated us and I remember the feeling of relief and surprise as we emerged into the sunlight.

We know of one who found this spot irresistible. In the late 18th century young Mary Ann Wodrow came to live in Little Cumbrae. Her family lived on the eastern, more sheltered side of the island, perhaps a little to the north of the present manor house. In 1785, at the age of 22, Mary Ann began to keep a diary. Her language is strong, clear, compact and punchy as she describes her activities and her surroundings, as on this day in August 1786:

*"**Fri.31**: After they were all gone to bed I went over to the Castle; I stood for some time gazing with a kind of soothing delight which touched my very soul. The sea was calm like a molten looking-glass, not even a breath to stir the down of the thistle which lightly floated here and there upon its surface. The beams of the broad full moon played beautifully upon it like a stream of fire, with the fish now & then rising above water. Their soft motion with the hum of the night fly, the blowing of whale, the wild note of sea fowl, the distant bark of dogs upon the mainland with the soft trickling of the water over the rocks all met the ear at once .... At last walked slowly home the long shadow stalking before me."*

The same stillness which soothed my Aunt Chrissie had been balm to Mary Ann's soul 150 years before.

There is some uncertainty as to when the castle was built. There are suggestions that it is David, son of Robert the Bruce, to whom the credit is due – he succeeded his father as King of Scots in 1329. His sister, Bruce's only daughter, Marjorie, married Walter, sixth High Steward of Scotland, and their son succeeded his uncle as King Robert II in 1371, when he was 55 years old. In the spring of 1375 he stayed for several weeks to enjoy deer-hunting and fishing. Again, in 1384 he had a holiday in his castle and doubtless several more visits. When he died in 1390, he in turn was succeeded by his son who, as King Robert III, also spent time there. From old records it seems that, in 1653, the castle was attacked and left in ruins by Oliver Cromwell's troops and since then it has not been inhabited. Our Royal family still holds the title of High Steward, Prince Charles being the 29th High Steward of Scotland.

While we were exploring the castle Mrs Urquhart had been busy. After tea, for the visitors' benefit, she showed us over the Manor House which she, as house-keeper and cook, kept in readiness for the owner's visits. From the original farmhouse it had been extended to an attractive, long, two-storey building with a tower that looked totally in place against the backdrop of grey rock and greenery. With three reception rooms, nine bedrooms, four bathrooms and a studio flat it was well equipped for entertaining.

The owner, Mr Ian Parker, had a great fondness for his island home and visited Little Cumbrae fairly frequently. There was a story that on returning from a voyage to the West Indies he ordered the captain to stop the ship close to Wee Cumbrae so that he could jump overboard and swim, the sooner to get to his beloved island. His ancestors had acquired plantations in the West Indies and traded in sugar and rum, with businesses in Greenock and Liverpool. As a consequence his father had been able to buy the island from the 17th Earl of Eglinton, whose family had owned it for the previous four centuries.

In the early 16th century the island was a Crown possession till in 1515 it was assigned to the 1st Earl of Eglinton, Hugh Montgomery – that name again! This was at first as supervisor, since the Hunters of Hunterston were proving "*nocht of power to resist the personis wha wasted*" the isle, and subsequently as owner. Except for a short period, when Mary, Queen of Scots appointed the Semples of Belltrees as guardians on her marriage to Darnley, it remained in the Eglinton family till Evelyn Parker, a yachting enthusiast, bought it in 1913 for the sum of £5,000 and set about renovating and improving buildings and grounds.

There was a large garden with vegetables and fruit trees. Interestingly, it was internationally-acclaimed Gertrude Jekyll who designed the original herbaceous borders. Her younger brother was a close friend of Robert

Louis Stevenson, who borrowed the family name for use in his novel *Dr Jekyll and Mr Hyde*. An enclosed garden was a lovely blend of golds with mauve and touches of red against the grey walls. Though the planting appeared random it was meticulously planned, as indicated by existing charts. The borders were more formal.

A walk northwards from the castle, along the shore, leads to just-discernible ruins of several cottages whose inhabitants were probably crofter-fishermen. A path to the left climbs and dips over rough terrain to the ruins of a chapel that keeps in memory a virgin nun, Vey Kumbra, who had once, long years ago, lived and worshipped here. Variously known as Saint Vey or Saint Beya, she is also referred to as 'the maiden'. There is some uncertainty as to when she lived – some think in the 9th century, but the more general opinion seems to be that she was an early 7th century follower of the teachings of Columba, an Irish monk who landed on Iona in 563AD and evangelised Dàl Riata, of which the islands of Arran, Bute and Cumbrae formed a part. It is possible that Columba himself may have visited Wee Cumbrae. Veya is reputed to have been escaping from a proposed marriage to a Danish prince, as she had already determined that her calling was to spread the teachings of Christ. She is also associated with Saint Maura or Mary whom she met at Lindisfarne. The two travelled to the Cumbraes and, while her friend set up a religious cell on Cumbra Mòr, Veya settled on Cumbrae Beag.

Only the foundation remains of what was a small two-roomed building, one half of which served as her dwelling, while she taught and worshipped in the little chapel. One would like to know more about this tantalisingly enigmatic woman and how she came to be on our little island. At her own request she was buried on the island. Her tomb lies a short distance to the north of the chapel and in following centuries her adopted island became a place of pilgrimage, with 1st November dedicated to her memory.

From the chapel the ground slopes down to Sheannawally Point, where heather and bracken give way to a meadow lush with plant life of great variety. The island has a long history of human occupation, stretching back to the Bronze and Iron Ages. At this ancient burying ground are to be found the remains of several cairns. In one of these, Hero's Cairn, were discovered a heavy sword with wrist-guard, armour dating back to Viking times and an iron helmet. Sheannawally (the old burying ground) is one of the names that show a Norse influence. In the 9th Century the Scots and Norsemen were engaged in a tussle over the Western Isles, including the Cumbraes and the Isle of Man, and for years the Vikings were masters. However, the Battle of Largs in 1263 settled the matter in favour of the Scots – who then, of course, had to contend with the English under Edward II. Robert the Bruce finally defeated the English king at Bannockburn in 1314.

Among the stones down on the shore are samples of the old red sandstone that underlies the volcanic rock that forms much of the island. From Sheannawally Point the land climbs in terraces up towards Tower Hill and on to the Sheughan Hills (hills of the fairies) and the bluffs of the south west where lie the Bennits (hill of nests).

Wee Cumbrae has its own little graveyard at Gull Point, overlooking the sea towards the south of the island. It is a lonely but lovely spot best visited on a sunny day. From the hilltop above the lighthouse a turn-off to the right leads to a grassy area, on a bluff, with a view down the wide estuary towards Ailsa Craig on the horizon. There stands the little walled grave-yard about four metres square. There is no gate, but there is a simple stile. We would sit on the low wall and view the few gravestones, perhaps seven or eight. One or two old stones are sunken and undecipherable but one dated 1774 captured our imagination, the grave of a fourteen-year-old girl named John Wodrow (perhaps Johan or Joan?) We liked to picture her, in happier times, sitting on the hill-side drinking in the beauty of the majestic Arran peaks. She had come to this spot to gaze out over the estuary, in the hope of catching a glimpse of the mast that would herald the return of her beloved, who captained a sailing ship. Day after day and week after long week she watched and waited till it became clear that she would never see him again. All hope gone she died, it was said, of a broken heart and was buried, according to her own wish, here where she had waved him off on his last voyage. We felt a strange kinship with this girl who had walked these familiar banks and braes so long ago. It was her younger sister, Mary Ann, who later kept the diary which throws such an interesting light on life on Wee Cumbrae over two hundred years ago. (see Epilogue on page 143)

A more recent stone bears an inscription to the memory of Evelyn Stuart Parker, who died in 1936 and is buried on the island he loved and for which he did so much. His widow, Mary, and the ashes of three sons would later be buried there.

Most poignant of all for us is the stone in memory of our friend, Alexander Urquhart, who on 29th September 1946 was drowned while returning to the island. Mr Ian Parker had been in residence for a few days and on Saturday Mr Urquhart had ferried him back to Fairlie on the mainland. The wind was moaning ominously so, after a hasty farewell, the boatman turned about and headed for home. Before he managed to pick up the shelter of the island the small boat got into difficulties, buffeted by the mounting seas. A passing fishing boat took in the situation and came swiftly to his aid. A towrope was secured to the small boat and progress made towards the lee of the island. Whatever happened next no one will ever know. The last the fisherman could recall was seeing our friend cut the rope and, when next they looked, both boatman and boat were gone. They could only surmise that, in the tricky situation, Mr Urquhart had feared being towed under and was compelled to cut the boat free.

The news of this tragedy was relayed to our side of the island the following morning, an idyllic day of blue skies, sunshine and an almost holy calm. The sense of shock and sadness was palpable.

All too soon came our time to start packing. The day of arrival or leaving was an occasion of great excitement, especially on Cumbrae. The *Torch* transported not only the personal items, but the families as well. The crane, which was perched on the edge of the cliff near the tower, came into its own on these days. One by one, heavy items were winched up or down the cliff face. Smaller articles were carried by way of the steps and this is where we children came in handy. Our only problem was trying to be in three places at once; supervising the crane, directing the carriers and, of course, minding our own business. It was all hustle and bustle and to-ing and fro-ing, just what children revel in.

We were to go to Toward Lighthouse in Argyllshire. It was with many a backward glance that we sailed away from our beloved island. It was a wrench for us all. We were growing up and things were changing, but the lighthouse was the link that rooted us in the past.

Chapter Nine

TOWARD POINT

The light from Toward Point lighthouse first shone out in 1812, just when Napoleon was embarking on his disastrous Russian campaign. It was built to make clear to ships from abroad the route to Greenock and Glasgow and to ease navigation between the Isle of Bute and the mainland. In 1877 the *Lady Gertrude*, on her way from Wemyss Bay to Rothesay, ran aground at Toward Point and it is easy to understand the need for a lighthouse on that spit of land. Though, at 63 feet, it is not so high as Cloch Lighthouse, the tower stands out prominently against a backdrop of the Cowal Hills. The grounds are set right by the sea where the view from the slipway is wide and, in the quiet of a summer evening, unusually tranquil. To stand there on the very tip of Toward Point, shimmering sea stretching into the distance, the Ayrshire coast away to the left, Bute off to the right and a sunset sky aglow, is an experience to treasure.

Toward, seven miles south of Dunoon on the Cowal peninsula, is an attractive little village with a church, a school and, just round the comer from the lighthouse, a shop-cum-Post-Office. As at the other two lighthouses, Toward's spacious grounds were enclosed within a white-washed wall. Our house was attached to the lighthouse, but the other two stood in their own garden. The path from our front door led down to the pebbly shore and its slipway.

Near our back door was the wireless room. It was from that room that contact was made with Cumbrae by wireless at the allotted times – if both remembered! I wondered what would happen if there was an emergency on Cumbrae between times. The lighthouse telephone was also in that room. If the men were not around we took any calls that came.

Like Cumbrae, Toward had its castle, the seat of the Lamont clan. It was about two miles beyond the village and was being used as an educational retreat for disadvantaged children from Glasgow. Children came for a fortnight at a time to enjoy fresh sea air and the freedom of roaming the woods and beach.

Set in woods just outside the village stood a mansion which, at that time, was a home for children who had been removed from their parents and were awaiting placement with foster parents. There was also, beyond the village, a turkey farm and every year when the festive season came round the farmer presented each of the lighthouse-keepers with the most succulent turkey we would ever taste.

We soon made friends with the village people. And there was one tremendous bonus – no more lodgings, no more homesickness. I attended the local one-teacher school, a solid stone building with high windows and a lovely big open fire. As well as the children from the village and surrounding farms, there were children from the mansion, who would appear suddenly and as suddenly disappear, though some were with us for months. Morning routine of Bible, sums, reading and spelling seldom varied. At dinner-time we locals made for home at full speed 'absolutely starving'. Straight away Mum would invariably hand me a bowl of soup to take over to Mrs Over-the-wall who lived alone. Though I protested: "I'll be late for school!" I never was. I suspect that, with retirement on the horizon, our teacher felt she deserved her lunch break even more than we did.

One of the treats our new playmates specially enjoyed was a visit to the light room – under Dad's watchful eye. While he busied himself with the log book he allowed us to climb the short iron ladder that led to the platform with the lantern and big concave mirrors. We giggled and exclaimed at the distorted images they threw back at us. However, we quickly learned to modify our capers in case we were unceremoniously ordered back to earth! Then we watched as the delicate gauze mantle was set on the bracket within its polished glass funnel, ready for use.

Mrs MacCallum was followed by a headmaster with a wife and cat and suddenly play-times and lunch breaks were, it was agreed, 'far too short'. In school he did not noticeably sparkle with wit and wisdom but, when they visited us of an evening, the talk around the fire was fast and free, with more than a sprinkling of laughter. It is amazing the things headmasters get up to when let out of school!

But the cat! The cat was another kettle of fish! Caspar was left in our care, or vice-versa, while the headmaster went on holiday – a heavy responsibility since he credited him with more than the combined wisdom of his pupils. Nevertheless, if it was fed with choicest fish and not sat on, we were confident that cat and we could survive. Come early evening, Caspar strutted to the door, demanded it be opened and streaked off, Dad surmised that puss had returned to the schoolhouse. We tore after him by bike and there was the culprit, disdaining to look our way. A fishtail soon enticed him and, with a concerted effort, we stuffed him into the saddlebag. No sooner were we home than he leapt clean out of the open window and vanished into the night. By dint of much over-indulgence he settled down, taking over Dad's chair and showing no inclination to terminate his holiday. Dad made sure that he did! And in time two sweet little girls arrived at the schoolhouse to put Caspar firmly in his place.

While I enjoyed the family atmosphere of the one-teacher village school, Flora and Joan travelled seven miles by bus to the town of Dunoon. The school bus picked up five or six pupils at the bus stop outside the village shop at 8.20am. The usual driver and conductress, a husband-and-wife team, were very good at waiting for the inevitable straggler – though at the price of a berating, which proved far more effective than any mother's threats! Who would have imagined then that, in a few years' time, bus-driving would be abandoned and they would be our good neighbours on Wee Cumbrae!

One Saturday, shortly after I had left for secondary school, word went round the village that one of the children from the mansion, Dugald Johnson – a quiet, always-smiling lad – was missing. The gloom of that day seemed almost to darken the sky. The police were alerted and the news media appealed for information, but no more was ever seen or heard of him. Years later a sandshoe was found in Glendaruel and there was speculation that it might have belonged to him, for it was thought that the little seven-year-old had relatives farther up the glen. Perhaps he had gone in search of them, met with an accident...?

Dunoon was a popular holiday resort, being accessible both by road via the 'Rest and be Thankful' and the Clyde steamers. The secondary school served the surrounding rural primaries, while pupils from as far away as Islay, Lochgilphead, Inverary, Minard, Karnes and Ardrishaig had the option of joining Dunoon Grammar School in 4th year. Among many characters was the late, highly respected John Smith, who became so prominent in the Labour Party. I remember our history teacher asking us what we all intended to do with our lives. Seriously, and without a trace of pomposity, John said that he wanted to be – no, was going to be – Prime Minister of Great Britain. As an audience to his wonderful debating skills, especially at mock elections, we did not doubt his ability to fulfil his ambition. Sadly, it was not to be – he died suddenly in May 1994 and is buried on the historic island of Iona. The genuine grief and shock throughout the country bore testimony to the esteem in which he was held.

Dunoon Grammar School was lively and forward-looking, with a memorable staff. Oswald

Brown, the headmaster, set the tone. A handsome man, he cut a distinguished figure striding along the corridor in his black gown, with a pleasant expression and watchful eye. Mr Gault, the inspiring Latin teacher, also gowned, was every inch the noble Roman senator. In contrast was the delightfully vague art teacher, with brilliantly-coloured cravat and clumpy boots. Nor should we forget the pretty young teachers who blushed scarlet whenever a bachelor colleague entered the room – it just may have had something to do with the prolonged fit of coughing which unfailingly afflicted the class!

The head of the English department, dignified and brooding, rejoiced in the name of Beltyer and was feared or admired depending on how well you knew your Shakespeare. Unfortunately, the maths department shared his love of the leather except for one soft-spoken Mull man. Faced with the task of inculcating the rudiments of geometry to a torpid third-year class, his incoherent exasperation was more terrifying than any hand-held implement. To this day the sight of an isosceles triangle can reduce me to a quivering jelly! Too many characters to name but all affectionately remembered.

Mum and Dad took an interest in our schoolwork. Mum was good with numbers and liked nothing better than the challenge of a difficult problem. In her unorthodox way she once succeeded in finding a solution that had baffled our class. Dad had a surprising grasp of Latin, learned in his village school. At exam time we had him test our vocabulary and were put to shame, managing to forget in five minutes what he had retained for forty years! As for French vocabulary, he pronounced the words phonetically and we, of course, had to respond in like manner – with the knock-on effect of being commended for our accurate French spelling. Nevertheless, I was fully 17 years old before I made the French connection to Mum's request to: "take the ration book and ask for 2lbs of sugar-in-loo-of-jam." Though the war was over, rationing was only gradually being phased out.

It was at Toward that a tortoise adopted us, so our budgie, Joey, now had a rival. Trotty could teach us children, and Joey, a thing or two about being slow and steady as well as being 'seen but not heard'. He settled in our flowerbed, until the wanderlust took him to the open road where he provoked intense interest. From the school bus we looked out for 'the lighthouse tortoise' inching his way along the verge. Would he ever reach Dunoon? Predictably he confounded us all by turning back on the outskirts of Innellan and took early retirement under the blue hydrangea bush in the front garden.

One great advantage of being on the mainland was that it was easier for friends to visit us. One afternoon Mum was busying herself arranging fresh flowers and generally titivating our cosy sitting room, in honour of two girls who were coming to stay for a few days. Delighted at the prospect of showing them round, playing on the beach and 'roly-polying' on the lawn, or 'going over our wilkies' as the local children termed somersaults, we waited on tenterhooks for the arrival of the bus. As it drew up, we scanned the few who disembarked – one of our neighbours and two old ladies, each holding on to her hat while managing a huge leather suitcase. Deflated, we ran home to announce that the girls had not arrived, only to hear, minutes later, Mum's delighted exclamation as she rushed out to welcome ... the two old ladies, who were probably not a day over forty! Thereafter we took the precaution of ascertaining whether expected guests were proper girls or just ladies.

One well-remembered visitor was a relative of our mother and she really was old. She had a certain aura about her, partly because she had been a 'Bible-woman' on the Isle of Lewis and partly because of her very lady-like manner, but mainly because she was a vegetarian, long before anyone could even spell the word!

Her strict vegetarian code proved a trial to us children. Our every waking moment seemed to be taken up with helping Mum grate carrots, wash lettuces, cut radishes, chop leeks, slice tomatoes, dice celery, snip parsley and pick chives and every other herb springing from the earth. Mum laughingly protested that we exaggerated, but we maintained that the half had not been told! As youngsters we only ever knew our old friend as 'the Lady of Edinburgh' and we found her fascinating. In later years, any illusions about being related to the aristocracy were dispelled when we learned that our 'Lady' was plain Miss Jessie Macdonald of Applecross and all the better for that.

Renovations were to be made to our house, so we moved in with Miss Kyle, a lady in the village, for three weeks. The wireless room was actually part of our house and the wireless was now to be relocated in the tower. When we returned to our home we were delighted to find that the wireless room was now our brand-new kitchen. It was fitted out with the latest green-enamelled Taycoette range while in our living-room the black range had been replaced by an up-to-the-minute fireplace.

One morning Mum and I were baking scones when we were startled by shouts of alarm and a clattering coming from the tower, then what sounded like roars of laughter. Out I went to investigate. Mr MacQueen had been going up to do a small paint-job on the tower. He missed a step and, in a torrent of Skye Gaelic, painter and paint-tin came rolling down together – the kind of thing you enjoy provided it's not you! While the keeper, dripping white, went off to face his (fortunately) patient wife, the two men got busy with paraffin and rags and mum and I returned to our scones.

Now that we had a road, it was time to have a car! For the princely sum of £100, Dad acquired an excellent Ford Popular and so proud of it was he that he kept it in as high a state of polish as the lighthouse brasses. It made local sightseeing jaunts so much easier than depending on buses.

We became familiar with many of the steamers criss-crossing between Rothesay, Dunoon, Innellan, Wemyss Bay, Largs, Skelmorlie and Gourock and in ensuing years became adept at manipulating the options and combinations as we travelled between home and school or college. There was nothing quite so heart-sinking as racing from the train down the pier, especially a long one as at Wemyss Bay, only to find the boat just drawing away. However, such occasions were rare and there was always an alternative that could be worked out. And missing the boat gave us time to admire the magnificence of Wemyss Bay station's canopy.

The steam-boat names became familiar – *the Marchioness of Graham*, the *Maid of Argyle*, and the paddle steamers such as the *Jupiter* and the *Columba*. The older paddle-steamers, dating from before the

Great War, included the *Waverley* (1899) the *Glen Rosa* and the *Talisman*. The *King Edward*, the first turbine steamer in the world, sailed the Clyde in 1901. The *Glen Sannox* with its two funnels belching smoke was a sturdy, reassuring favourite. The *Waverley* of course as the last surviving paddle steamer is everyone's favourite, ours too, who travelled on her so often. We liked to explore each on our travels, venturing down below where the engines were at work, similar to the huge rolling cylinders in the engine-rooms at our lighthouses. To sit up in the bows with the soft breeze or whipping wind was exhilarating and relaxing at the same time.

It was the advent of steamers in the previous century that led to the Fair Fortnight, when the good citizens of Glasgow downed tools and sailed 'doon the watter' for a week of exuberant enjoyment as they baffled their hosts with their unique brand of humour. And in the latter half of the century those Glaswegians who could afford them bought houses in the Clyde resorts to which they could escape during the smog of summer. At Toward, in one such large Victorian villa, lived three gracious ladies; Greta, Geraldine and Sophie Riddell were the last remaining members of their family. Their father had been a minister in Glasgow. Mum and occasionally one of us would be invited for afternoon tea, served in their large, elegantly-furnished drawing room before a glowing fire. Silverware glinted on starched lace-and-linen. There was a formality about the enjoyable occasion that was evocative of a bygone age, a peep into the past as it were, and yet with the formality went a down-to-earth involvement with the everyday present.

In 1882 their oldest brother, William, a pupil at Bellahouston Academy, had injured his knee during a football match. Sadly the incident was to prpove fatal and he died nine months later. During those months little three-year-old Sophie would cheer him with her artless chatter. His mother kept a diary which she sent regularly to her sister in America, recounting 'his perfect peace and rest of mind' during those months of intense pain and suffering. Not meant for publication, it nevertheless later appeared in print. In the Preface the writer recommends to young people this account of William "looking calmly and hopefully on the approach of death, through simple faith in Christ". The Riddell ladies gave Mum a copy of *A Bright Sunset*, still a family treasure.

Lighthouse keepers had three weeks' holidays a year and it was the principal keeper's responsibility to suggest a reliable man from the vicinity to fill in. So John Ruxton, the village shopkeeper, became our relief keeper. He enjoyed this nine-week annual stint and was solidly dependable. One afternoon he went for a nap before going on duty, reminding his wife to be sure to waken him in good time for lighting up. Dusk came and went and darkness proper fell. At last, John's gentle little wife woke her husband: "I think it's maybe time for lighting up, John." One glance at the darkness outside and John made for the tower, pulling on his uniform as he ran. From the light-room Dad, having long since put things in motion, could hear him panting up the stairs, berating himself: "I've let you down! You'll never trust me again! Oh, what have I done, what have I done … !"

At Toward we were once more reunited with Archie Sinclair, his wife and six-year-old son Kenny, to our mutual delight. One beautiful afternoon, as he and Dad were loitering around the slipway, admiring the placid sea and commenting on boats, tides, the national situation, world affairs and the wayward ways of budgies, they spotted far out a boat that appeared to be empty. "Look Roddy! That boat's drifting! It'll soon be in the path of the steamers!" Grabbing oars they were soon making headway towards it – but never quite catching up. Always it was that tantalising bit ahead, no matter how hard they rowed.

Then Archie felt something: "Roddy! There's water! Water's coming in!" With no time to lose, rescue was forgotten and they made for shore, now so far away. And still the water seeped in and Archie was struggling to keep pace with Dad's rowing. They had no means of getting rid of the water, which was ankle deep by now, and the shore seemed as far off as ever. Then Dad said, "Your cap, Archie! You bail out and I'll do the rowing!"

Off came the cap and Archie bailed and bailed, while Dad pulled at the oars. And still the water level rose, but the intake was slowed down sufficiently for them to make landfall as the boat was on the point of going under. I was coming down the path as the two were squelching wordlessly up the slipway, too exhausted to even glance at me.

One winter's night Dad was on duty in the tower. It was bitterly cold and he walked up and down, up and down to keep his circulation going. On watch there was time for contemplation, for taking a breath of fresh air, but not for falling asleep – an indulgence which would lead to instant dismissal. Dad stepped out on to the balcony. To his consternation he noticed that the Wee Cumbrae light was no longer giving its familiar signal. It had stopped! Had the keeper fallen asleep, taken ill, had an accident? What should he do? By law Dad should have reported this to the authorities immediately. Trouble lay in store for the defaulter – and trouble for himself, if he failed to report the matter. He felt his dilemma acutely. Time crawled by and still no light. Then the light began to flash as if a giant hand were whirling the platform round. It was no giant – just the keeper back from dreamland!

No reference was made to the incident, until some years later when Dad was retiring. Then he nonchalantly told the keeper in question the phenomenon of the 'weird flashes' that one night emanated from the Cumbrae light. The guilty cat-napper was stunned to realise that his lapse had been observed. He told how he had sat down 'for a few minutes' and woke to silence. The light! Grab the winder! Then out to the balcony, to see the lights of a ship disappearing beyond Holy Isle. The machinery had stopped with the beam facing the hill, not the sea. The two men – cat-napper and distant watcher – had spent an uneasy few days, but now they could laugh about it.

But that day was still to come. Ten years had passed at Toward and we were beginning to scatter. I was the youngest and I, alone, was left at home. It was time for our next posting – to Little Cumbrae.

Chapter 10

HOME AGAIN

So it was just Mum, Dad and I who sailed into Little Cumbrae in the hazy sunshine of a late summer's day. As we stepped ashore the island seemed to envelop us in its welcome embrace. Certainly there were changes, not least from my perspective – mountains had become molehills and miles yards. But some things never change: porpoises tumbling in a clear blue sea; the lonesome call of a solitary wren winging its way home; the rhythmic slipslap of wavelets caressing the rocks below. The setting sun that brought our first day to a close shed a golden glow that warmed us through and through. It was so good to be *home*!

Thanks to two little girls I had the happy privilege of reliving my early childhood days. Catherine-Anne and Margaret were the five-year-old daughters of our two neighbours. Together we wandered the island, swam in Steadholm Bay, guddled in rock pools and chased one another round and round the lighthouse balcony. Of those last few blessed days random memories remain – mothers sitting down at Steadholm Bay, backs against a high rock where it sloped down to the grassy shingle, its ledges and hollows offering tufts of wild pinks, walks down to North Landing on an evening of 'clear shining after rain'. And, as I extended a helping hand to these youngsters, I recalled the willing hands that had reached out to help me over rocks, out of bogs, through waist-high bracken. Happy blest indeed!

Then it was time for me to leave home too. After a lifetime devoted to their family, Dad and Mum might well have relished the prospect of some time and space for themselves. I was not convinced of that as they waved me off to join the ranks of students in the bustling city of Glasgow. Mum was a gifted letter-writer and we all looked forward to her graphic epistles, which roamed over everything from issues of national importance to how well – or otherwise – the hens were laying.

My first visit home to Little Cumbrae from college began inauspiciously. Weighed down with an enormous leather suitcase and a vast array of packages I faced a journey by tram, train, steamer and motor boat. It was rather late to regret the moment of madness that led me to volunteer to take the college hamster for the Christmas break, so when the paddle steamer *Waverley* tied up at Millport pier I was more than a little fractious. Maybe that is why I took such exception to Dad's insensitivity towards my travelling companion. As he stowed bits and pieces under canvas he muttered about having to find 'a corner for the rat'. A bad start!

Hardly had we loosed the ropes than a squall blew up. By the time we reached the Tan the boat was rocking alarmingly and Dad was transferring his pipe from his mouth to his inner pocket. Suspicious that he was eyeing the 'rat' – or perhaps me – in Jonah-like speculation, I kept the hamster's cage firmly between my feet and wished for the safety of home. Thanks to Dad's skill we managed to turn around and eventually anchor safely at Bruce's Castle on the east side of Wee Cumbrae. From there, we trudged over the hill, carrying as much as we could. One of the keepers came to relieve us of some of our burdens.

The following day was mirror-calm and we sailed the boat home round the south end of the island. That restored my equilibrium and I settled down happily to help with preparations for the homecoming of the rest of the family. Dad, meantime, went about securing the door of the hamster's cage with much the same tackle as was used to moor the *Torch*. My return journey would have been infinitely easier had he allowed the creature enough scope to make a successful bid for freedom.

The lighthouse was undergoing yet another face-lift. Electricity was being introduced to our island. Five years previously work had begun on laying a cable on the sea-bed from Great Cumbrae to supply power to the lighthouse, fog-horn and houses and, subsequently, overhead to the other side of the island. The electricians Emil and Willie lodged with us for some weeks. Emil was a charming Pole, a clever engineer, who was to accomplish the electrification of the light. He had fought for Britain during the war and had later married and settled in Scotland. Willie, his assistant, had a pawky sense of humour, so between the two we were well entertained. The work was completed in four weeks in May 1957. So in our homes it was goodbye to paraffin lamps and the wonder of light at the touch of a switch.

As I took up my first appointment, Dad entered his last year of lighthouse service. As a newly-fledged teacher I taught in the Easterhouse district of Glasgow. On Friday afternoons a colleague and I exchanged classes. He was to take my seven-year-olds for a music lesson while I had I the unenviable task of presenting 'the life cycle of the earwig' in such a way as to enthral his class of 50 eleven-year-olds, most of whom were boys, some as big as I and all considerably cheekier. Five minutes into the lesson they made it abundantly clear that their interest in the humble earwig was marginally less than mine. So, without preamble, I embarked on a wholly unrelated topic – lighthouses. The level of interest rose dramatically and, by afternoon's end, we had produced a colourful frieze to decorate the back wall. The class teacher graciously accepted my apology for changing course. From years of experience he assured me that I need have no illusions – the first buzz of the bell would obliterate all memory both of lighthouses and earwigs.

Inevitably, time came for Mum and Dad to bid farewell to a way of life that had served them well and to which they had given loyal commitment. Our upbringing in the lighthouses had been interesting and varied. If there was a downside, it was that we missed the opportunity of cementing friendships forged in early schooldays. By way of compensation-in our childhood beside the busy and bonny Clyde we had lived among a people who had the enduring qualities of kindness and warmth, enhanced by a unique brand of humour.

In what consists the attraction of a lighthouse-keeper's life? Being awakened from sleep at 3am on a night of icy winds, to step out within minutes in the gale? But to counterbalance that is the joy of dawn on a fresh spring morning, while the world sleeps! To some extent, how one views such a life must depend on personality. It is difficult to pinpoint the appeal of such a life for families on Cumbrae. All were caught up in the rhythm of watches, regular but changing with the seasons, and inevitably became sensitive to the subtleties of wind, sea and sky.

There is the sense of community. A similar sense of a shared outlook and life-style probably goes with many occupations, but it is perhaps enhanced when three lighthouse families live enclosed within surrounding walls. Then, in the case of the CLT, there is the wider family of the different lighthouses, the Clyde Lighthouse Trust and the still wider community of lighthouse dwellers in general. Add to that smart uniform, substantial accommodation, superb scenery and, on Cumbrae, the appeal of living on an island – little wonder the memories echo with a tinge of times that were truly special.

I recently rediscovered a letter from Archie Sinclair which evokes memories of comradeship and contentment and which encapsulates the blend of light-heartedness and seriousness with which the keepers approached their work:

"…. I remember when we came back with the boat full of water & scared out of our wits, altho' if we had any wits we would have stayed ashore. One man said: "We were very frightened for you both, but I suppose you chaps will take it all in the day's work." Your Dad replied: "Yes, we are used to this kind of work!" Our knees were knocking so bad that we could hardly walk up to our houses …. I also remember the time when Mr Watson rang up on the phone & your Mum took the call and said: "Roddy is over at Archie's plucking blackcurrants." She didn't mention that she was speaking on the phone and when Watson rang up the following day I said I would get Roddy: "He is over in my garden plucking blackcurrants." I won't repeat what Watson said about the blackcurrants …Tell your dad we still remember the good old days…."

In 1974 automation brought an end to 217 years of dutiful 'lighting up' by the keepers of Clyde Lighthouse Trust. For the principal keeper on Wee Cumbrae, our old friend Archie Sinclair, and his wife Mary, it was a fitting farewell as they made their home by the river they knew so well. In 1997 there was a final change when solar panels were installed. Sadly, the splendid buildings and grounds were abandoned to the elements, a melancholy reminder of what was once a happy community doing vital and fulfilling work. Progress, one supposes.

As for ourselves, once we had settled in our new abode with its attractive garden, Dad made it his first task to remove the nameplate on our front gate, replacing it, letter by letter, with STEADHOLM. Every month the postman brought a copy of the seaman's *Living Links*, and every year a hamper full of luxuries arrived labelled 'With best wishes for the New Year from the trustees of the Clyde Lighthouses Trust'.

Looking back fondly on the sunset days of our much-loved parents, a quotation from JC Ryle comes to mind:

I am like a ship about to unmoor and put to sea.
All on board is ready.
I only want to have the moorings cast off that
fasten me to the shore
And I shall then set sail and begin my voyage...

An elegant liner passes Cumbrae from the busy Clyde.

The town of Millport on Big Cumbrae, and the pier steps from which I jumped aboard the boat on the day of my great escape.

Mum and Dad, Roderick and Elizabeth MacCuish (née MacDonald)
after their retirement, in the 1970s.

Epilogue – Mary Ann's Diary

*(The diaries of Mary Ann Wodrow are in the care of
the Museum of the Cumbraes at Millport. Extracts
are used by kind permission of the archivists.)*

Our happy childhood on Wee Cumbrae made it seem
that the island was ours alone, but of course there have
been many before and since who have treasured the
same landscapes and similar experiences. Mary Ann's
journal paints a vivid picture of life on the island in the
late 18th century, shortly before the present lighthouse
was built. She was five years old, her sister Joan was
seven and brother Peter eleven when the family came
to live on the Isle, as she called it.

She has an interesting background. Her father was
a grandson of James Wodrow, Professor of Divinity in
Glasgow University. His son, Robert, the historian and
author of *The History of the Sufferings of the Scottish
Church*, had pastoral charge of Eastwood Church near
Glasgow and was popularly known as 'Honest Wodrow'.
He had 16 children, some of whom became ministers of
the Church of Scotland, Mary Ann's father – also Robert
– being one of them. Patrick, of Tarbolton Church near
Ayr, features in one of Robert Burns' poems as 'Auld
Wodrow', while James was minister in Stevenson and
later became Principal of Glasgow College.

So the young family had uncles, aunts and cousins almost without number! After his first wife died leaving him with four children, her father married Ann Ruthven from Beith. In 1767 he retired through ill health from his charge near Glasgow and moved to Wee Cumbrae. The sea breezes seem to have restored his health somewhat and he lived another 17 years. When he died in 1784 he was buried in the little graveyard beside his young daughter. The widowed mother thought it was time to leave the island and Peter was inclined to agree, but Mary Ann would not hear of it.

Some months later the 22-year-old girl began to keep a diary. It was to be an honest account of daily happenings and in strong, clear language, compact and punchy, we have her view of life on the isle with its hopes and hazards. She has a way with words; water falls with a '*soft purling noise*' over the rocks and she is displeased with herself for '*active idleness*' while '*time is whirled away*'. Not surprisingly, in view of the wrecks and accidents that she witnessed, she is ever aware of the brevity and uncertainty of life and given to pondering its mysteries: '*but I am bewildering myself...*'

Home was on the eastern, more sheltered side of the island, perhaps a little to the north of the present manor house. What strikes us is that there were many more comings and goings than in our day and traffic was with the Ayrshire mainland, rather than with

Millport, which at that time was little more than a village of fewer than 60 houses. Her diary records a surprising number of names, including that of David Pollock, the lighthouse-keeper. On Friday evenings there were dances up at the lighthouse, children and adults joining merrily in the reels together. There are frequent references to a 'smoke', which was the signal for someone to be met on the opposite shore and off the boat would go.

There is an intriguing contrast between the social scene on the mainland and the practicalities of life on the island, where we find her wheeling pebbles from the shore and unloading lime to build a garden wall for, although they sometimes had a maid, she was ready to turn her hand to anything required. Her interests were many. She enjoyed reading, music, drawing and painting – especially the wild flowers that grew in abundance around her. She appreciated good furniture and works of art and, in what leisure she had, she maintained a wide correspondence.

Weather permitting, there were sails over to church in Hunterston. Weather not permitting they stayed at home and kept the Sabbath much as we did in our day except that Mother and guests read a sermon (or two) aloud to the company. The young girl appreciated the writings of John Newton, the former galley slave turned minister, who was at that time the rector of St Mary Woolnoth Church in a fashionable part of

London and composer of many hymns including the well-known *Amazing Grace*.

> *Amazing grace, how sweet the sound*
> *That saved a wretch like me*
> *I once was lost, but now am found*
> *Was blind, but now I see.*

The diary covers a period of almost three years. In the spring of these years she and her mother spent several months on the mainland visiting friends and relatives. In early 1786 Mary Ann was seriously ill for about five weeks.

A few entries from her diary give a flavour of life on the isle over two hundred years ago.

MARY ANN WODROW'S DIARY

1785

JANUARY 1st: In the evening had the young people in at tea as usual. When I was a child this was a great entertainment to me.

Mon 10th: Played upon the guitar and wrote some in the evening. The children came in and planted themselves round the fire; amused at their innocent chat.

Thurs 13th: To Hunterston and visiting friends in Kilbride, Springfield and Bogston on way to Stevenston.

FEBRUARY 4th: A most pleasant ride to Beith.

Sat 12th: With Peter over to the Isle for two hours; pleased to show the improvements made to the house since Father's death.

Sun 13th: Heard of death of Mrs Ferry's son and called on her between sermons.

Tues 22nd: Got a post-chaise to Paisley; the stage to Glasgow. Stayed 5 weeks in Glasgow.

MARCH: Arrived in Paisley, got a horse and had a disagreeable ride – very windy with rain, and the horse ungovernable; warm welcome at Beith.

APRIL: Invited to a Ball; as many, mostly children, as made 20 couples for a country dance.

Wed: Went to a play, "She Stoops To Conquer." How bewitching these entertainments.

Fri: Adieu to Beith; we came in sight of the sea, like meeting with a friend; spent 2 or 3 days in Hunterston.

MAY 2nd: Came home; the banks white with blossom.

JUNE: Miss Kerr went over with us to the Sacrament. Two excellent sermons from Mr Adams.

JULY 5th Tuesday: Peggy Wodrow came and right glad was I to see her. Mother says that our minds have been cast in the same mould.

AUGUST 14th Sunday: James Hogart's wife died in childbed.

SEPTEMBER 7th Wed: Mrs Miller & I set over Miss Mary; the wind came against us; much difficulty getting home; arrived much fatigued at 8 at night.

Fri 9th: Ball in Mr Miller's – had the pleasure of seeing all the children happy – got everything our own way, choosing our favourite tunes.

Tues 20th: A boatful of sailors from Kilbride.

OCTOBER 2nd Sunday: a most pleasant seat at North Bank; the sky was of that beautiful deep blue which is peculiar to the harvest season, tinged with fine dusky clouds – bright sun and soft murmur of the sea.

Sat 8th: Drew a bunch of brambles with the blossom which looked exceeding well.

Mon 31st: Shocking news; two vessels on shore at back of the Isle; a fine Brig and a very large sloop overturned and dashed against the rocks. Two surgeons lost and a little boy, brother of the Capt of the sloop; gave lodgings that night to a poor fellow, a schoolmaster.

NOVEMBER 1st Tues: 2 boats with gentlemen from Greenock and Glasgow.

Wed 9th: All hurry and confusion – every hour we saw new faces.

Tues 15th: The gentlemen came in to take leave of us; thanked us for our attention.

Sun: Mrs Wylie and I went to visit the boy's grave – poor youth dashed upon the raging surge – no friend near to help.

1786

JANUARY, 1786: The morning of this Year seems to smile upon me. I took a little walk up the barn Brae – what a pleasing aspect – the fine dark green of the ivy with reflection of the sun upon the icicles which hung in many a fantastic shape from the rocks.

Coloured a picture of Milton – a lively animated face with fine eyes.

FEBRUARY 2nd Thurs: Set out about 10 o'clock and left Mrs Murray in tears promising to count the hours of our absence.

Wed 15th: We went aboard the *Eglantine* & Peter showed us his books.

Mon 27th: Peter took leave of us; recollected the agreeable conversations by night at the fireside & sighed to think of the uncertainty of human events. My headache still continuing but I strove to drive it off.

(*For the next four weeks she was in a "high fever".*)

APRIL 27th Thurs: Left all our kind friends. Got two smokes kindled and a boat soon arrived; a kind welcome from all our honest neighbours.

MAY 1st Mon: Began to get the garden cultivated; people sending away their sheep, the lambs left crying in vain for their mothers.

Fri 12th: The Tacksmen (landlord's representatives) came to look at the houses etc.

Sat 13th: Finished my wool and twined it etc.

Sat 27th: Heard of a King's wherry which was lost with 15 or 16 men near the Big Cumbra.

Sun 28th: Read some letters of Newton about his conversion.

Mon 29th: We saw a vessel full of people searching in vain for the corpses of their friends.

Tues 30th: Pulled a large bunch of trefoil flowers which we greatly admired; tried to draw one of them but found it impossible to imitate the beautiful curled leaf & fine snowy fringe; what a trifling childish mind must I have. I blush at the recollection but will not suppress it. This little book must be sincere.

JUNE Tues 21st: Mary Dickie came to be our servant.

Tues 28th: A boat in the evening- a throng house but we got beds for all except Mr D.

JULY 17th Monday: Just heard a piece of melancholy news – Mr Alexander's death. He fell from the ship's mast and was never seen.

AUGUST 11th: After dinner we took a sail round the Isle – went ashore and saw the Broad Cave. In the evening I went to bring round the boat.

SEPTEMBER 26th Tues: Mr Ritchie has died suddenly of fever – only about 8 days sickness; a shock to all his friends.

Fri 29th: They went over to the burial.

OCTOBER 16th Mon: Gathered a decanter of bramble berries for my Mother as she is fond of them.

Tues 17th: Built our little peat stack, returned with a load. The parts I have to act! Now I go tottering beneath my burden; will soon perhaps be in a riding habit with the air of never having known what work was; now I'm the rough hardy sailor; then drawing on my gloves appear as one who shrinks at a blast; this time I was recompensed by a blazing fire and the tea things ready.

Thurs 19th: In the evening caught 3 fish & returned with a lapful of sticks.

Tues 24th: The youngest Mr Archbald, our new tacksman drank tea with us. There seems to be much simplicity & good nature in his character but no ideas above the way of life to which he has been accustomed. Plain rusticity.

NOVEMBER 7th Tues: Over to Millport for quarrying instruments; night was beautiful; drank tea with B Tyre.

Thurs 16th: A storm of northeast wind; men could not get away, a small misfortune if our meal etc. were not very near.

Sat 25th: At the lighthouse today having not seen it since it was repaired.

Thurs 30th: My Mother went to Hunterston. It was with much reluctance that I thought of being alone, but as yet have been disappointed to the better.

DECEMBER 1st Fri: James Archbald came in and sat with me till it was pretty late – there is but very little in his conversation though nothing assuming, which makes him at least tolerable. Sabbath; Much struck by a sermon of Newton's; "Come unto me all ye who labour and are heavy laden and I will give you rest." Read through 2 or 3 following which were extremely good; excellent author.

Fri 8th: All day making puddings and a most disagreeable employment it was.

Sat 9th: I was much struck the other day with the sight of a ship that went in past dreadfully shattered & one of her masts away. Where, ah where is my dear brother? Perhaps at this moment – but I will not indulge the painful idea. Gracious God be thou his guide.

Mon 11th: Dreadful storm of thunder and hail; afraid the window would have been shattered to pieces; Most dreadful flash of lightning.

Thurs 14th: I heard that Jon's family had no meal – & grudged to sit down to a plentiful table by myself so sent for Jennet and treated her.

1787

JANUARY 1st: In the evening Dr Pollock,
A Robison, his wife and 3 Archbalds drank tea with
us; Wm. sensible, Jon with a desire to please, James
with a pair of fine eyes, glow of youth & innocence &
had he received the polish of education ... ..

Sat 6th: To Kilbride; Fog so thick that after rowing
some time we came in to the very place from which
we had set out; got home about midnight.

Sat 30th: Home. Mother away a few hours later in
the boat that brought me.

APRIL: Forgot to mention the night I was in
Greenock heard that the beauteous Miller was no
more; had got command of a vessel and on his first
voyage was lost with the whole crew; his poor mother
.... Scarce a 12-month since 5 young men have been
cut off; every serious thought is put off till tomorrow;
tomorrow comes and still we trifle on.

MAY 6th Sabbath: Mother was persuaded to take a
walk north below the bank. She was struck with the
rich profusion of flowers.

Mon 7th: The Archbalds are not to build any new
houses. Jas has given up all thought of living on the
Isle; his Father is giving land to him; my heart foolish
and capricious; begin to suspect myself of some secret

wish to attract a heart which I had once vanity enough to think below my notice.

Sabbath 20th: This afternoon took a walk up to the grave. I looked at the little spot in the comer & recollected that it was Duncan Alexander who had assisted me to delve it.

JUNE 2nd Sat: Busy all day hoeing and weeding; felt the force of that simile where the mind is compared to a garden.

Tues 12th: to Fairlie; dined in Mr Lang's; saw the new edition of Burns poems with his picture - an animated penetrating face, the brow a little heavy.

Wed 27th: Went all round the island in a boat; left them at the Long-bay & came home to make tea.

Thurs 28th: The Arch'ds came to clip the rest of the sheep.

AUGUST 13th Mon: Rec'd 13 letters – luxury indeed.

Fri 17th: Mr Miller sailed for Virginia; what will this Isle turn to – a desert, I fear.

Sabbath 26th: Went over; the morning very coarse; we were late, part of the sermon being over.

Mon 27th: A fine day. Went over again. Put on my brown silk, and pink petticoat etc. Must dress sometimes to let people see that one can!

Fri 31st: After they were all gone to bed I went over to the Castle; I stood for some time gazing with a kind of soothing delight which touched my very soul. The sea was calm like a molten looking-glass, not even a breath to stir the down of the thistle which lightly floated here and there upon its surface. The beams of the broad full moon played beautifully upon it like a stream of fire, with the fish now & then rising above water. Their soft motion with the hum of the night fly, the blowing of whale, the wild note of sea fowl, the distant bark of dogs upon the mainland with the soft trickling of the water over the rocks all met the ear at once .... At last walked slowly home the long shadow stalking before me.

SEPTEMBER 2nd Fri: A storm which continued all day. The highest sea that ever I saw or that any could remember; thought the side of the house would have been blown in. What a dreadful scene to those who are at sea.

Thurs 4th: Had a large washing. I took my light printed gown and some shifts etc. up to the Long Bank which occasioned my going much up and down.

Sabbath 30th: A blowy day. None got over. Another month of my life now draws near a close & with it I must end this little book. Alas! How trifling but if upon review it but taught me to be humble it would be well ..... Sep'tr 30, 1787

Two years later, in August Mary Ann married James Archbald – her "fair rustic" – and they set up home on the Isle. Their first child, Robert, born on June 26th 1790, lived for only a week and was buried in the little graveyard overlooking the sea. Twins arrived on 10th July 1791 and James followed in March 1793, by which time the new lighthouse was being built.

If only she had gone on to record those days and we could know her reaction to the undertaking, and especially her opinion of the 19-year-old Robert Stevenson who stayed with them while overseeing the work! Did they appreciate one other? How interesting it would be to have been an eavesdropper around their cosy hearth!

In 1807 the Archbald family emigrated to America. Mary Ann's mother died in 1814 and Mary Ann in 1841.